CW00645773

Italy
1815–1943

Derrick Murphy ■ Terry Morris

Published by Collins
An imprint of
HarperCollinsPublishers
77–85 Fulham Palace Road
Hammersmith
London
W6 8JB

Browse the complete Collins
catalogue at
www.collinseducation.com

© HarperCollinsPublishers Limited
2008

10 9 8 7 6 5 4 3 2 1

ISBN-13 978 0 00 726869 6

Derrick Murphy asserts his moral
rights to be identified as the author
of new content in this work.

All rights reserved. No part of this
publication may be reproduced,
stored in a retrieval system, or
transmitted in any form or by any
means, electronic, mechanical,
photocopying, recording or
otherwise, without the prior written
permission of the Publisher or a
licence permitting restricted copying
in the United Kingdom issued by the
Copyright Licensing Agency Ltd.,
90 Tottenham Court Road, London
W1T 4LP.

British Library Cataloguing in
Publication Data
A Catalogue record for this
publication is available from the
British Library

Edited by Graham Bradbury
Commissioned by Michael
Upchurch
Design and typesetting by Derek Lee
Cover design by Joerg
Hartmannsgruber, White-card
Map Artwork by Tony Richardson
Picture research by Celia Dearing
and Michael Upchurch
Production by Simon Moore
Indexed by Malcolm Henley, Henley
Indexing
Printed and bound by Printing
Express Ltd, Hong Kong

ACKNOWLEDGEMENTS
Every effort had been made to
contact the holders of copyright
material, but if any have been
inadvertently overlooked the
publishers will be pleased to make
the necessary arrangements at the
first opportunity.

Bonacci for the extract from *Roma tra
Londra e Berlino: La politica estera
fascista dal 1930 al 1940* by Rosaria
Quartararo (1980). Cambridge
University Press for the extracts from
*Italy in the Making, 1846 to 1st
January 1848* by G Berkeley (1936)
and *Hitler's Italian Allies: Royal Armed
Forces, Fascist Regime, and the War of
1940–1943: Royal Armed Forces,
Fascist Regime, and the War of
1940–1943* by McGregor Knox
(2000). Columbia University Press
for the extract from *The Economic
History of Modern Italy* by S.B.
Clough (1964). Constable for the
extract from *Mussolini* by Jasper
Ridley (1997). Harcourt Publishers
Ltd for the extract from *The Origins
of Totalitarianism* by Hannah Arendt
(1973). Hodder Arnold for the
extracts from *Mussolini* by R.J.B.
Bosworth (2002) and *Italy (Inventing
the Nation)* by *Nicholas Doumanis*
(2001). Longman for the extracts
from *Italy in the Age of the
Risorgimento, 1790–1870* by Harry
Hearder (History of Italy series,
1983) and *Modern Italy 1871–1982*
by Martin Clark (History of Italy
series, 1984). Methuen for the extract
from *Cavour* by Denis Mack Smith
(1985). Orion Publishing Group for
the extracts from *Garibaldi and the
Making of Italy* (Weidenfeld &
Nicholson, 1911) and *Mussolini* by
Denis Mack Smith (Weidenfeld &
Nicholson, 1981). Oxford University
Press for the extract from *The
Political Life and Letters of Cavour
1848–1861* (1930). Routledge for the
extract from *Fascist Italy* (1969).
University of Nebraska Press for the
extract from *Italian Fascism: Its
Origins and Development* by
Alexander De Grand (1989). Van
Nostrand for the extract from *Cavour
and the Unification of Italy* (1961).

The publishers would like to thank
the following for permission to
reproduce pictures on these pages.
T=Top, B=Bottom, L=Left, R=Right,
C=Centre

akg-images 34, 35, 54, 78, 88,
96,122,123; akg-images / ullstein
bild 103; Private Collection,
Archives Charmet / The Bridgeman
Art Library 77; © Hulton-Deutsch
Collection/Corbis 85; 89;
© Bettmann/CORBIS 105, 109, 121;
Getty Images 84, 87; Mary Evans
Picture Library 23; © World History
Archive / TopFoto57; Unknown 55,
97, 99.

Contents

Study and examination skills

This section of the book is designed to aid Sixth Form students in their preparation for public examinations in History.

- Differences between GCSE and Sixth Form History
- Extended writing: the structured question and the essay
- How to handle sources in Sixth Form History
- Historical interpretation
- Progression in Sixth Form History
- Examination technique

Differences between GCSE and Sixth Form History

- The amount of factual knowledge required for answers to Sixth Form History questions is more detailed than at GCSE. Factual knowledge in the Sixth Form is used as supporting evidence to help answer historical questions. Knowing the facts is important, but not as important as knowing that factual knowledge supports historical analysis.

- Extended writing is more important in Sixth Form History. Students will be expected to answer either structured questions or essays.

Structured questions require students to answer more than one question on a given topic. For example:

> (a) Why did revolutions break out in Italy in 1848?
>
> (b) How far was the failure of the revolutions due to divisions among the revolutionaries?

Each part of the structured question demands a different approach.

Essay questions require students to produce one answer to a given question. For example:

> To what extent was the unification of Italy due to foreign intervention?

Similarities with GCSE

● **Source analysis and evaluation**

The skills in handling historical sources, which were acquired at GCSE, are developed in Sixth Form History. In the Sixth Form, sources have to be analysed in their historical context, so a good factual knowledge of the subject is important.

● **Historical interpretations**

Skills in historical interpretation at GCSE are also developed in Sixth Form History. The ability to put forward different historical interpretations is important. Students will also be expected to explain why different historical interpretations have occurred.

Extended writing: the structured question and the essay

When faced with extended writing in Sixth Form History students can improve their performance by following a simple routine that attempts to ensure they achieve their best performance.

Answering the question

What are the command instructions?
Different questions require different types of response. For instance, 'In what ways' requires students to point out the various ways something took place in History; 'Why' questions expect students to deal with the causes or consequences of an historical event.

'How far' or 'To what extent' questions require students to produce a balanced, analytical answer. Usually, this will take the form of the case for and case against an historical question.

Are there key words or phrases that require definition or explanation?
It is important for students to show that they understand the meaning of the question. To do this, certain historical terms or words require explanation. For instance, if a question asked 'how far' a politician was an 'innovator', an explanation of the word 'innovator' would be required.

Does the question have specific dates or issues that require coverage?
If the question mentions specific dates, these must be adhered to. For instance, if you are asked to answer a question on Mussolini and foreign policy it may state clear date limits, such as 1922 to 1940. Also questions may mention a specific aspect such as 'domestic policy' or 'foreign affairs'.

Planning your answer

Once you have decided on what the question requires, write a brief plan. For structured questions this may be brief. This is a useful procedure to make sure that you have ordered the information you require for your answer in the most effective way. For instance, in a balanced, analytical answer this may take the form of jotting down the main points for and against an historical issue raised in the question.

Writing the answer

Communication skills
The quality of written English is important in Sixth Form History. The way you present your ideas on paper can affect the quality of your answer. Therefore, punctuation, spelling and grammar, which were awarded marks at GCSE, require close attention. Use a dictionary if you are unsure of a word's meaning or spelling. Use the glossary of terms you will find in this book to help you.

The quality of your written English will not determine the Level of Response you receive for answer. It may well determine what mark you receive within a level.

To help you understand this point ask your teacher to see a mark scheme published by your examination board. For instance, you may be awarded Level 2 (10–15 marks) by an examiner. The quality of written English may be a factor in deciding which mark you receive within that level. Will it be 10 or 15 or a mark in between?

The introduction

For structured questions you may wish to dispense with an introduction altogether and begin writing reasons to support an answer straight away. However, essay answers should begin with an introduction. These should be both concise and precise. Introductions help 'concentrate the mind' on the question you are about to answer. Remember, do not try to write a conclusion as your opening sentence. Instead, outline briefly the areas you intend to discuss in your answer.

Balancing analysis with factual evidence

It is important to remember that factual knowledge should be used to support analysis. Merely 'telling the story' of an historical event is not enough. A structured question or essay should contain separate paragraphs, each addressing an analytical point that helps to answer the question. If, for example, the question asks for reasons why Mussolini became prime minister of Italy in October 1922, each paragraph should provide a reason for his rise to power. In order to support and sustain the analysis evidence is required. Therefore, your factual knowledge should be used to substantiate analysis. Good structured question and essay answers integrate analysis and factual knowledge.

Seeing connections between reasons

In dealing with 'why'-type questions it is important to remember that the reasons for an historical event might be interconnected. Therefore, it is important to mention the connections between reasons. Also, it might be important to identify a hierarchy of reasons – that is, are some reasons more important than others in explaining an historical event?

Using quotations and statistical data

One aspect of supporting evidence that sustains analysis is the use of quotations. These can be from either a historian or a contemporary. However, unless these quotations are linked with analysis and supporting evidence, they tend to be of little value.

It can also be useful to support analysis with statistical data. In questions that deal with social and economic change, precise statistics that support your argument can be very persuasive.

The conclusion

All structured questions and essays require conclusions. If, for example, a question requires a discussion of 'how far' you agree with a question, you should offer a judgement in your conclusion. Don't be afraid of this – say what you think. If you write an analytical answer, ably supported by factual evidence, you may under-perform because you have not provided a conclusion that deals directly with the question.

Source analysis

Source analysis forms an integral part of the study of History.

In dealing with sources you should be aware that historical sources must be used 'in historical context' in Sixth Form History. This means you must understand the historical topic to which the source refers. Therefore, in this book sources are used with the factual information in each chapter. Also, specific source analysis questions are included at the end of most chapters.

How to handle sources in Sixth Form History

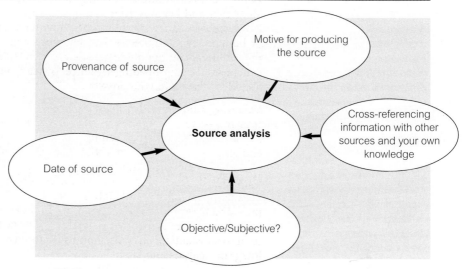

In dealing with sources, a number of basic hints will allow you to deal effectively with source-based questions and to build on your knowledge and skill in using sources at GCSE.

Written sources

Attribution or Provenance and date

It is important to identify who has written the source and when it was written. This information can be very important. If, for instance, a source was written by Count Cavour in 1860, this information will be of considerable importance if you are asked about the usefulness (utility) or reliability of the source as evidence of Piedmontese policy in that year.

It is important to note that just because a source is a primary source does not mean it is more useful or less reliable than a secondary source. Both primary and secondary sources need to be analysed to decide how useful and reliable they are. This can be determined by studying other issues.

Is the content factual or opinionated?

Once you have identified the author and date of the source, it is important to study its content. The content may be factual, stating what has happened or what may happen. On the other hand, it may contain opinions that should be handled with caution. These may contain bias. Even if a source is mainly factual, there might be important and deliberate gaps in factual evidence that can make a source biased and unreliable. Usually, written sources contain elements of both opinion and factual evidence. It is important to judge the balance between these two parts.

Has the source been written for a particular audience?

To determine the reliability of a source it is important to know to whom it is directed. For instance, a public speech may be made to achieve a particular purpose and may not contain the author's true beliefs or feelings. In contrast, a private diary entry may be much more reliable in this respect.

Corroborative evidence

To test whether or not a source is reliable, the use of other evidence to support or corroborate the information it contains is important. Cross-referencing with other sources is a way of achieving this; so is cross-referencing with historical information contained within a chapter.

Visual sources

Cartoons

Cartoons are a popular form of source used at both GCSE and in Sixth Form History. However, analysing cartoons can be a demanding exercise. Not only will you be expected to understand the content of the cartoon, you may also have to explain a written caption – which appears usually at the bottom of the cartoon. In addition, cartoons will need placing in historical context. Therefore, a good knowledge of the subject matter of the topic of the cartoon will be important.

Photographs

'The camera never lies'! This phrase is not always true. When analysing photographs, study the attribution/provenance and date. Photographs can be changed so they are not always an accurate visual representation of events. Also, to test whether or not a photograph is a good representation of events you will need corroborative evidence.

Maps

Maps which appear in Sixth Form History are predominantly secondary sources. These are used to support factual coverage in the text by providing information in a different medium. Therefore, to assess whether or not information contained in maps is accurate or useful, reference should be made to other information. It is also important with written sources to check the attribution and date. These could be significant.

Statistical data and graphs

It is important when dealing with this type of source to check carefully the nature of the information contained in data or in a graph. It might state that the information is in tons (tonnes) or another measurement. Be careful to check if the information is in index numbers. These are a statistical device where a base year is chosen and given the figure 100. All other figures are based on a percentage difference from that base year. For instance, if 1870 is taken as a base year for iron production it is given the figure of 100. If the index number for iron production in 1900 is 117 it means that iron production has increased by 17% above the 1870 figure.

An important point to remember when dealing with data and graphs over a period of time is to identify trends and patterns in the information. Merely describing the information in written form is not enough.

Historical interpretation

An important feature of both GCSE and Sixth Form History is the issue of historical interpretation. In Sixth Form History it is important for students to be able to explain why historians differ, or have differed, in their interpretation of the past.

Availability of evidence

An important reason is the availability of evidence on which to base historical judgements. As new evidence comes to light, an historian today may have more information on which to base judgements than historians in the past.

'A philosophy of history?'

Many historians have a specific view of history that will affect the way they make their historical judgements. For instance, Marxist historians – who take the view from the writings of Karl Marx the founder of modern socialism – believe that society has been made up of competing economic and social classes. They also place considerable importance on economic reasons in human decision making. Therefore, a Marxist historian of fascism may take a completely different viewpoint to a non-Marxist historian.

The role of the individual

Some historians have seen past history as being moulded by the acts of specific individuals who have changed history. Mazzini, Garibaldi and Cavour are seen as individuals whose personality and beliefs changed the course of 19th-century Italian history. Other historians have tended to 'downplay' the role of individuals; instead, they highlight the importance of more general social, economic and political change.

Placing different emphasis on the same historical evidence

Even if historians do not possess different philosophies of history or place different emphasis on the role of the individual, it is still possible for them to disagree because they place different emphases on aspects of the same factual evidence. As a result, Sixth Form History should be seen as a subject that encourages debate about the past based on historical evidence.

Progression in Sixth Form History

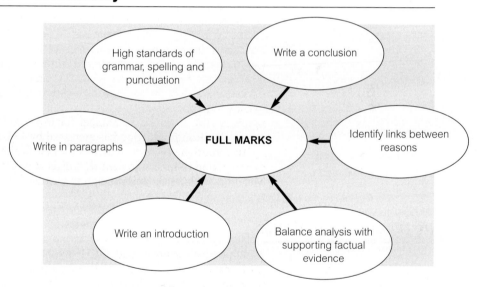

The ability to achieve high standards in Sixth Form History involves the acquisition of a number of skills:

- Good written communication skills
- Acquiring a sound factual knowledge
- Evaluating factual evidence and making historical conclusions based on that evidence
- Source analysis
- Understanding the nature of historical interpretation
- Understanding the causes and consequences of historical events

- Understanding themes in history which will involve a study of a specific topic over a long period of time

- Understanding the ideas of change and continuity associated with themes.

Students should be aware that the acquisition of these skills will take place gradually over the time spent in the Sixth Form. At the beginning of the course, the main emphasis may be on the acquisition of factual knowledge, particularly when the body of knowledge studied at GCSE was different.

When dealing with causation, students will have to build on their skills from GCSE. They will not only be expected to identify reasons for an historical event but also to provide a hierarchy of causes. They should identify the main causes and less important causes. They may also identify that causes may be interconnected and linked. Progression in Sixth Form History will come with answering the questions at the end of each sub-section in this book and practising the skills outlined through the use of the factual knowledge contained in the book.

Examination technique

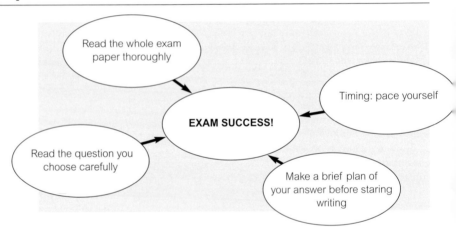

The ultimate challenge for any Sixth Form historian is the ability to produce quality work under examination conditions. Examinations will take the form of either modular examinations taken in January and June or an 'end of course' set of examinations.

Here is some advice on how to improve your performance in an examination.

- Read the whole examination paper thoroughly
  Make sure that the questions you choose are those for which you can produce a good answer. Don't rush – allow time to decide which questions to choose. It is probably too late to change your mind half way through answering a question.

- Read the question very carefully
  Once you have made the decision to answer a specific question, read it very carefully. Make sure you understand the precise demands of the question. Think about what is required in your answer. It is much better to think about this before you start writing, rather than trying to steer your essay in a different direction half way through.

Revision tips

Even before the examination begins make sure that you have revised thoroughly. Revision tips on the main topics in this book appear on the Collins website:

www.collinseducation.com

- Make a brief plan
Sketch out what you intend to include in your answer. Order the points you want to make. Examiners are not impressed with additional information included at the end of the essay, with indicators such as arrows or asterisks.

- Pace yourself as you write
Success in examinations has a lot to do with successful time management. If, for instance, you have to answer an essay question in approximately 45 minutes, then you should be one-third of the way through after 15 minutes. With 30 minutes gone, you should start writing the last third of your answer.

Where a question is divided into sub-questions, make sure you look at the mark tariff for each question. If in a 20-mark question a sub-question is worth a maximum of 5 marks, then you should spend approximately one-quarter of the time allocated for the whole question on this sub-question.

1 Italy 1815–1943: A synoptic overview

Key Issues

- How far did Italian nationalism change between 1815 and 1943?

- How important were individuals in shaping Italian history between 1815 and 1943?

- To what extent were Italian affairs affected by foreign powers between 1815 and 1943?

BETWEEN 1815 and 1943 Italy and Italian affairs were of central importance to European history. In the period 1815 to 1848, Italy was one of the major centres for liberal revolutionary activity. In 1820–21, 1830–32 and 1848–49, revolts, by liberals, occurred in several Italian states. In every case, the liberals were defeated.

However, between 1850 and 1861 Italy moved towards political unity. The key Italian figures in this process were the Piedmont Prime Minister, Cavour, and the liberal revolutionary, Garibaldi. Cavour's aim was to make Piedmont the dominant North Italian state. Garibaldi wanted an Italian Republic. Yet, without foreign assistance neither aim was likely to be achieved. The process of unification, therefore, had more to do with France than through the efforts of Italians themselves. The French involvement in the war of 1859 was the turning-point in the move towards unification. French victory in that war unleashed forces in Italy which allowed Cavour and Garibaldi to overthrow the Italian state system and create an Italian state by 1861. The completion of the process came in 1870 with the acquisition of Rome.

To many the unification of Italy was the triumph of liberal nationalism. However, from 1870 to 1915 liberal rule in Italy failed to offer a stable political system. Italy remained economically backward. Italian attempts to be regarded as one of Europe's major powers fell far short of expectations.

The decision to enter the First World War in 1915 on the side of the Allies was another turning-point in Italian history. The war caused considerable problems for Italy. Over 750,000 lost their lives, the economy was badly damaged, and Italian aims in the war were largely unrealised by the peace treaties of 1919–1920. And without the war, fascism would not have developed as a mass movement.

The political and economic chaos which followed the war was exploited effectively by Mussolini and his fascist movement. From 1922 to 1943, Mussolini gave Italy a degree of political stability which had not existed since

1. Produce a timeline, identifying what you think were the five most important dates in Italian history between 1815 and 1943.

2. Who do you regard as the most important Italian political leader in the period 1815 to 1943? Give a reason for your choice.

3. How did Italian nationalism change from 1815 to 1943?

unification. But it came at a price. Mussolini established a dictatorship, and his foreign policy aims eventually led to Italy's entry into the Second World War on the side of Nazi Germany. This proved to be a disastrous decision, and by 1943 Italy was invaded by Allied troops.

It had been foreign troops, in the form of France, that had helped to unite Italy in 1859, and in 1943 it was foreign troops (British and American) who led to Mussolini's fall from power.

Nationalism, in the period 1815 to 1870, was seen as a modernising force. It helped remove the autocratic rule of Italian monarchs and created a unified state. Under Mussolini, nationalism became associated with dictatorship and led directly to Italy's humiliating defeat in the Second World War. With Mussolini's fall in 1943, Italy descended into civil war between 1943 and 1945.

2 Italy, 1815–1848

Key Issues

- How widespread was unrest in Italy 1815–1848?

- Why did attempts at revolution before 1848 fail?

- How extensive were liberalism and nationalism in Italy in this period?

2.1 What was Italy like, 1815–1820?

2.2 What were the causes and results of the revolutions of 1820–1821?

2.3 Why, and with what results, was there further unrest in Italy in 1831?

2.4 What was the contribution of Mazzini to the movement for change in Italy after 1831?

2.5 What influences were promoting nationalism in Italy, 1831–1846?

2.6 What was the effect of Pope Pius IX's election on Italy in 1846?

2.7 Historical interpretation: How widespread was nationalism in Italy before 1848?

2.8 Why did Italian nationalists consider the prospects of Italian freedom and statehood so promising in 1846–1848?

2.9 How was Austria able to reassert its conservative influence over Italy?

Framework of Events

1814–15	The Vienna Settlement. A system of separate states, mostly controlled by their former ruling houses, is re-established in Italy
1820	Revolution breaks out in Kingdom of Naples
1821	Revolution begins in Kingdom of Piedmont-Sardinia. Austrian troops are used to destroy both revolutions
1824	Charles Albert becomes King of Piedmont-Sardinia
1831	Revolutions in Modena, Parma and the Papal States are crushed by Austrian troops. Mazzini founds 'Young Italy' (a nationalist society) in Marseilles
1843	Publication of Gioberti's *Primato* arguing for a federation of Italian States under the Pope
1844	Publication of Balbo's *Delle Speranze d'Italia* arguing for national leadership by the Kingdom of Piedmont-Sardinia
	Attempted revolution in Calabria (Naples) by Bandiera brothers
1846	Election of Pope Pius IX, widely regarded as a reformer, rouses liberal hopes
1847	Cavour and Balbo found *Il Risorgimento* ('The Resurrection'), a nationalist newspaper
1848	Revolutions occur in many Italian States.

Overview

DURING the period 1815–1848, Italy was not a unified country (see map on page 16). Prince Metternich, the Austrian Chancellor, once referred to the area as 'a geographical expression'. This was nothing new. Italy had been disunited since the fall of the Roman Empire in the 6th century although, during

Vienna Settlement: A peace settlement for Europe after the French wars and Napoleonic domination, 1814–15.

Conservative : This implies keeping things as they are.

Illiterate: Unable to read or write.

the Napoleonic period, the number of States had been reduced. However, in accordance with the principles of the **Vienna Settlement** – to reduce French influence and to recreate, as far as possible, the stability of the 18th century – the settlement of 1815 returned Italy to a system of separate states, each under its own ruler and system of government. This arrangement suited the Austrians as it kept the area relatively weak. It also enabled it to exercise a good deal of influence over the peninsula and to control the spread of revolutionary ideas. In its **conservative** aims, Austria was helped by most of the Italian rulers, who were noted for their resistance to change, and by the undeveloped economic state of most of Italy at this time.

The peninsula suffered from long-standing economic backwardness, made worse by its geography and climate. Ninety per cent of the population was dependent on some type of farming, many were **illiterate** and the power of the Roman Catholic Church was strong. By the 1840s, both economic and political progress was being made in some states, notably Piedmont-Sardinia, but most Italians in this period accepted their lot.

For the educated minority, a society in which they had no say in political affairs, no legal means of influencing the decisions of their governors, and little, if any, freedom to express themselves in speech or writing was less acceptable. Consequently, it was this middle-class group that led the movement for change. Working in the utmost secrecy because of the strict censorship, the Carbonari and other societies, inspired a number of risings in the 1820s and 1830s. By the 1840s, the activities and writings of Giuseppe Mazzini, a cultural revival, scientific congresses, as well as the publication of a number of progressive books and journals, in the freer atmosphere of this decade, encouraged the literate to consider what Italy's future path should be.

The desire for political freedom became entwined with a desire for independence from Austria and, in some cases, with a desire for a unified Italy. However, none of these wishes was crowned with success in this period. Although the various risings of the 1815–1848 period brought some minor victories, as rulers fled or were compelled to grant reforms, most were reversed in the reaction that followed. The

1. Which of the factors in the mind map aided greater Italian unity in the period from 1815 to 1848? Give reasons for your answer.

2. Which factors were obstacles to Italian unity in the period from 1815 to 1848? Give reasons for your answer.

3. How strong was the desire for Italian unity by 1848?

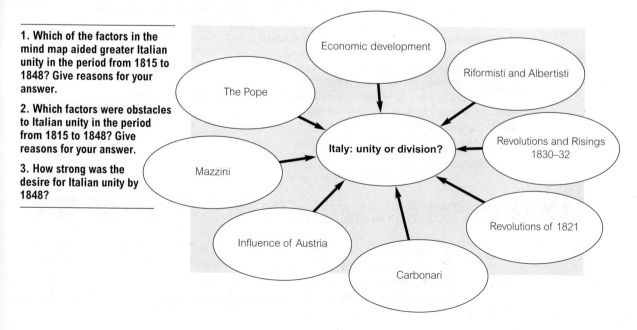

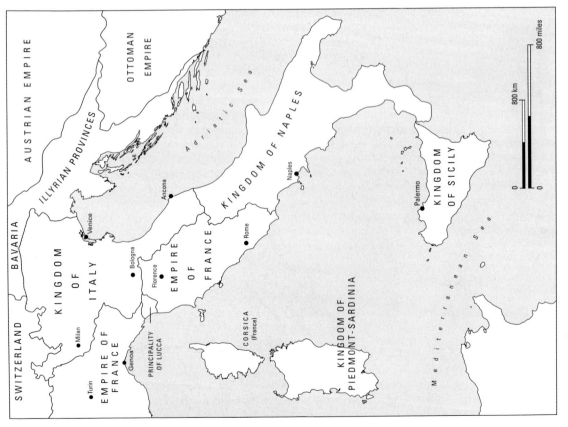

> **Charles Albert I (Carlo Alberto) (1798–1849), King (1831–1849)**
> He became the great hope of the liberals after 1821 when he was unexpectedly thrust into power as a regent for his uncle Charles Felix. He made vague liberal pronouncements, which were interpreted as a sign of liberal sympathy, although he never really made it clear whether he supported the revolutionaries or not. This flaw was to make him a poor leader after his accession in 1831. He was so hesitant, he became known as '*il re Tentenna*' ('King Wobble'). In 1833 he had 12 men killed following a conspiracy, but after 1837 he carried out extensive reforms in Piedmont-Sardinia, including the reform of the army. He was ambitious and devious. He was certainly not a liberal and, despite several nationalist speeches, his main interest was to extend the power of Piedmont-Sardinia at the expense of the Austrians. Only in 1848 did he finally grant a constitution to his Kingdom.

1. Compare the map of Napoleonic Italy (left) with that of Italy in 1815.

2. Which areas of Italy have changed the most?

only lasting improvements were those granted freely by reforming monarchs such as Charles Albert of Piedmont-Sardinia. This was a time of frustrated hopes for the leaders of the insurrections, but some of the ideas that were to form the basis of the later unification of Italy were laid down in this period.

2.1 What was Italy like, 1815–1820?

What ideas influenced the Italian Settlement at Vienna in 1815?

During the years of French rule, 1796–1814, there had been considerable political and social change in Italy. Not only had the number of states been reduced, the French legal code had been introduced and communications had been improved. Many Italians benefited from wider economic and social contacts both within the peninsula and outside. The position of the old aristocracy had been weakened, the peasants' burden was eased by the abolition of **feudal taxes**, and the educated middle classes enjoyed positions of responsibility in administration and law. Consequently, this 'middling' group of people, in particular, benefited considerably from French rule. They saw the advantages of the greater freedom and unity that it brought to the peninsula.

Feudal taxes: The dues which peasants owed to their Lords for the right to farm their plots.

However, the victors – Russia, Austria, Prussia and Great Britain, who met at Vienna in 1815 – regarded some of these changes as highly dangerous. They believed Italy needed protection, not only from French ambition, but also from such dangerous, modern ideas as liberalism and nationalism. Metternich feared disruption within his own multi-national Empire, should such ideas make headway in Italy. He believed it was his job to 'extinguish the spirit of Italian unity and ideas about constitutions'. The Vienna Settlement, therefore, involved removing French influence, restoring legitimate rulers where possible, and placing Austria in a position of control. The Italian nationalist, Mazzini, was to write later, 'throughout Italy, one stroke of the pen erased all our liberties, all our reform, all our hope'. It is true that many of the more progressive French reforms were swept away with the restorations of 1815. However, to be fair to the Vienna statesmen, even among those Italians who had benefited from Napoleonic rule, there were very few people who even thought in terms of Italian unity in 1815.

What territorial and governmental changes were made in Italy in 1815?

The Vienna Settlement created five main groups of states in Italy (see the map on page 16). Of the four republics that had existed in Italy before the

Napoleonic wars – Venetia, Genoa, Lucca and San Marino (a tiny city state) – only the latter survived. The other areas were returned to strong personal rule. (A table of the Italian rulers of this period, beginning with those mentioned below, is on page 22.)

The Kingdom of the Two Sicilies (sometimes known as the Kingdom of Naples and Sicily)

The most southerly Kingdom was restored to Ferdinand I, a member of the royal line of Spanish Bourbons. He had spent the war years in his island province of Sicily, protected by the British navy. In 1815, he was restored to the mainland part of his Kingdom, Naples, and received the title 'King of the Two Sicilies'. His **domains** which were dry, hot and malarial, were the most economically undeveloped in Italy. His subjects were mainly poverty-stricken and highly superstitious peasants. Ferdinand abolished the constitution granted to the area in 1812, and set himself up as an absolute ruler, supported by the higher clergy. His rule was unenlightened. One of his own ministers referred to the executioner as 'the Crown's first servant'. Court and government were corrupt, there was strict censorship, expenditure on social projects such as schools and communications was reduced in an effort to meet financial difficulties, and nothing was done to counter the underlying economic problems.

The Papal States

Pope Pius VII, who had been held as a prisoner by Napoleon, returned from exile in France to recover his former possessions. He was reinstalled in the Vatican Palace in Rome, and enjoyed direct rule over the province of Rome and the two **Papal legations**, Romagna and Umbria. This area was collectively known as the Papal States. Initially, the French greeted Pius' return with some enthusiasm and sympathy, after his harsh imprisonment. He was certainly respected for his spiritual leadership throughout the peninsula. However, his return also meant the return of the power of the clergy. Under his guidance, the Catholic Church became an instrument of conservative and oppressive government. The French system of centralised administration was retained, but priests regained authority. Five **Papal legates** and 12 **priest-delegates** ran the 17 provinces that made up the Papal States. There were a few lay members on local advisory councils, known as 'congregations' (abolished in 1824), but otherwise control was firmly back in the hands of the clergy, most of whom were firmly against any changes brought by the French and any measure of reform. French law was abolished; those who had worked with the French were removed. Laws, which had introduced uniform weights and measures, street lighting and vaccination against smallpox, were cancelled. The Jews were confined to a **ghetto**. The **Inquisition** was reintroduced and torture was used to extract confessions from any whose ideas were viewed as subversive. The 'Zelanti', a powerful Catholic group, blocked virtually all suggestions of reform whether concerning justice, education or economic affairs.

The Central Duchies

In the central north were a number of duchies controlled by dukes or duchesses. The Vienna Settlement made some complicated provisions for the smaller duchies, which gradually fell under the rule of the larger ones (as can be seen from the map of Italy in 1815 on page 16). The major duchies of the period 1815–1847 were Tuscany, Modena, Parma and Lucca. These were generally better governed than the states of the south although, even here, the historian Franklin Ford commented that 'autocracy and extortion were the twin principles of government'. Duke Ferdinand III of Tuscany, a cousin of the Austrian Emperor, was never excessively heavy-handed. However, another cousin, Duke Francis IV of Modena, was far

Domains: Areas over which someone or something has control or influence.

Pope: The head of the Catholic Church. In the 19th century the Pope fulfilled two roles. He was both a spiritual (religious) leader, God's representative on earth, in the eyes of all Roman Catholics throughout the Christian world, and a temporal (earthly) ruler with control over the Papal States.

Papal legations: Areas in which the Pope's officials were in control.

Papal legates/priest-delegates: These were offices held by those who represented the Pope in the different areas of the Papal States.

Ghetto: An area, usually on the outskirts of a city, where Jews were forced to live.

Inquisition: A committee that investigated peoples' private lives. Its job was to discover those who denied the teachings of the Church and, traditionally, it used torture and underhand methods to extract confessions. It was hated as a symbol of repression and an infringement of personal liberty.

more oppressive. They both ruled their duchies with the help of an extensive secret police network modelled on that of Austria. In Parma, Marie-Louise, daughter of the Austrian Emperor and former wife of Napoleon, was regarded as more liberal in attitude. French law was retained, judges were permitted independence and this was the only state in Europe where Jews were able to enter the civil service. However, Marie-Louise, who was later to marry the Austrian General, Count Neipperg, never escaped her Austrian connections. The tiny state of Lucca, which had formerly been a republic, became a duchy under the rule of Maria Louisa of the House of Bourbon. However, when the Bourbons retook Parma on the death of Duchess Marie-Louise in 1847, Lucca reverted to Ferdinand III of Tuscany (see table of Italian rulers on page 22).

The Austrian Empire in Lombardy and Venetia

Francis I, Emperor of Austria, assumed direct control of Lombardy and Venetia, the two richest Italian provinces. The administration here was far better than in Naples or the Papal States, and opportunities were wider too. Education was compulsory to the age of 12 and to some extent trade and communications benefited from the Habsburg connection. However, improvements were also offset by conscription and heavy taxation. Although they formed only an eighth of the population of the Empire, they contributed one-quarter of the imperial revenues. Furthermore, direct Austrian rule meant a loss of jobs for those lawyers and administrators who had enjoyed positions of responsibility under the French. Whereas, formerly, the language of administration had been Italian, after 1815 it became German, and the new government only employed Austrian judges, civil servants, police and army officers. Freedom of speech and the press were curtailed and students were forbidden to read such dangerous subjects as 'Modern History' at university. Although the surveillance and censorship was not as oppressive as has sometimes been suggested, there was an intense resentment of the Austrians among those most affected by the changes.

The Kingdom of Piedmont-Sardinia (also known as 'Sardinia', 'the Kingdom of Sardinia' or 'Piedmont')

In the north-west, Victor Emmanuel I of the House of Savoy headed the Kingdom of Piedmont-Sardinia. He had continued to rule the island part of his kingdom, Sardinia, throughout the Napoleonic period. However, in 1815, he regained his mainland possessions, which were considerably increased in size. The two provinces of Savoy and Nice were confirmed as part of his possessions and the former republic of Genoa was added. The King ruled from his capital, Turin (in Piedmont), which was the most economically developed part of his kingdom. His government was reasonably honest and taxation was not too oppressive, thanks to a fair trading revenue. However, one of the King's first actions was to abolish the French legal system and to return lands, tax exemptions and privileges to the nobility and Church. He was fanatically anti-French, removing French 'improvements', such as roads and lighting, and dismissing all those civil servants who wrote an 'R' in the French manner. He also imposed censorship, and a permit was needed to read foreign newspapers. The King brought back internal **customs duties**, reinstated the religious orders, and confined Jews to ghettos. His subjects were obliged to attend **mass** and **confession** at least once a month. Beards and long hair, considered revolutionary, were forbidden.

Customs duties: Taxes charged on goods entering a country. Also known as tariffs.

Mass/confession: Two sacraments, or acts, which are essential for true Catholics. Mass involves participation in the religious service commemorating Jesus' Last Supper, at which bread and wine are turned into the body and blood of Christ. Catholics are also required to confess (tell) their sins (misdeeds) to a priest in order to receive forgiveness. Without this, they cannot enter the kingdom of Heaven.

What was the social and economic state of Italy in 1815?

Compared with Britain and France, Italy was economically backward in 1815. Although it had been a wealthy trading nation in the 15th and 16th centuries, commerce had since lost favour with the nobility. With 90% of the population still working the land, the economy was almost entirely based on agriculture. To make matters worse, the population growth – from 13 million in 1700 to around 18 million in 1800 – had left many peasants short of land. Farming methods were primitive and inefficient, and the fields were cultivated under semi-feudal conditions. Although Napoleon had abolished feudal taxes, some were revived in 1815 and around half the peasantry still had to work for their landlords in the north, and an even greater proportion in the south. There was little industry, and virtually none in the undeveloped southern states. Industrial development was hindered by, among other things, poor transport. Geographically, the mountains of the Apennines cut Italy in two from north to south, and there were few good roads. The King of Piedmont-Sardinia even closed the road over Mount Cenis because the French had built it. Travel between states was not encouraged either. The Duke of Modena once declared 'travellers are Jacobins' and he would not allow stage coaches to cross his territories.

The new rulers restored the customs barriers that had been swept away in Napoleonic times, making commerce between states difficult and costly. The river Po, Italy's main navigable river, was divided into 22 sections by customs points.

In the towns, society was divided between the professional middle classes (lawyers, civil servants, writers, intellectuals and students), the 'financial' middle classes (bankers, merchants, industrialists and engineers), the workers (skilled craftsmen and manual workers) and the unproductive classes (beggars, road sweepers, petty criminals and the like). Few of these were better off after 1815 although, for most of the towns' workers, life did not change a great deal. They continued to live and work in crowded and unhealthy conditions. It was the small but influential middle class that was most obviously affected. Censorship and surveillance caused a good deal of resentment, while many lawyers and administrators lost work with the abolition of French law codes and practices.

What factors were preventing political progress in Italy after 1815?

Apart from the conservative rulers and the economic constraints, there were a number of other factors hampering progress in Italy in these years.

- There was a good deal of political apathy. Every day living was far more important for most Italians than political affairs, and they were resigned to their lot. There was widespread illiteracy and in the south, in particular, much poverty, ignorance and superstition. For the majority of people, 'patriotism' meant loyalty to a state, not to Italy as a whole. Men would describe themselves as, for example, Neapolitans or Tuscans rather than Italians,

- Even language differed between states and this hindered communication. French was spoken in Piedmont-Sardinia, Latin was the official language of the Papal States, while the Austrian rulers used German. The ordinary people also spoke in quite different dialects, often incomprehensible outside their own region.

- Although it had lost power under Napoleon, the Roman Catholic Church regained its influence after 1815. This was particularly marked in the 'Kingdom of the Two Sicilies', Piedmont-Sardinia and the Papal States. Superstition and fear of the Church were rife in the south, where the clergy enjoyed a great deal of local power. In the Papal States, Church law was state law and impinged on every subject. In Piedmont-Sardinia, the Catholic Church was freed from taxation, had full control over education and ran its own law courts. Throughout

Italy, Church teaching stifled economic, political and intellectual developments. Preaching a message of conservatism and acceptance, the teachings of the Church reached far more ears than the words of the liberal reformers.

- The influence of Austria was felt everywhere. Apart from its direct control in Lombardy and Venetia, Austrian influence in Italy was maintained through its network of family alliances and military dependence. The Dukes of Tuscany and Modena and the King of Piedmont-Sardinia were all cousins of the Emperor. The Duchess of Parma and the Queen of Naples were both his aunts. The Pope also looked to Austria for support, as it was the most important of the Catholic states of Europe. Naples and Tuscany entered into direct alliance with Austria, promising not to alter their forms of government without consultation. Although the Papal States, Tuscany and Piedmont-Sardinia refused to do this, Metternich set up a 'postal convention', whereby the foreign correspondence of each state had to pass through Austria and was thus subject to Austrian scrutiny and control. Metternich's highly-organised police system and the Austrian spy network ensured widespread surveillance. He maintained an Austrian minister at each court, with agents and informers reporting private conversations and gossip, as well as infiltrating suspected revolutionary groups.

**'Holy Alliance'**: This came to represent an alliance in favour of the suppression of revolution.

- Since the major powers of Europe had drawn up the 1815 settlement, they had a vested interest in maintaining it, and were not interested in the injustices of the petty rulers. Russia and Prussia were united in the **'Holy Alliance'** of 1815 with Austria, and hated anything which hinted at revolution. Britain and France were slightly more sympathetic but, in the immediate aftermath of 1815, were in no position to help even if they had wanted to.

What new attitudes and ideas were influencing Italy from 1815?

Although the vast majority of Italians had little concern for wider issues of government and reform, new political ideas did begin to spread among the educated middle classes after 1815. This was partly a result of the experiences of the Napoleonic period and partly a reaction to the conditions imposed on Italy after 1815. The idea of a *Risorgimento* of the Italian nation had first been suggested in the 18th century. It implied that a 'reborn', unified Italy might once again become great and powerful, as it had in the glorious years of Ancient Rome. Supporters of this idea shared two different beliefs.

*Risorgimento*: Literally meaning 'rebirth'. This was the term given to the growth in Italian patriotic and nationalistic feeling during the 19th century.

- Nationalism was a sense of loyalty to the State. This included a pride in its shared background and a belief that, only in a united country, could the people truly flourish. In the liberal revolutionary, Mazzini's view the nation was 'the God-appointed instrument for the welfare of the human race'.

- Liberalism was the belief that personal freedoms, such as freedom of thought and speech, as well as freedom from arrest and imprisonment without trial, were among the most important rights of man. Liberals believed only representative government could preserve these. The more extreme liberals were sometimes known as radicals. They favoured republicanism, a form of government with no monarch at its head.

Both of these beliefs clearly appealed to those who had tasted unified and representative government in Napoleonic times. However, those of sufficient education, wealth and ambition to seek change, were still small in number. The keenest supporters came from the professional middle classes, university students, lawyers, teachers and doctors. A number of civil servants and disgruntled army officers left unemployed with the ending of the Napoleonic era, were also attracted to the cause.

How were the new ideas and attitudes spread?

Freemasons: A secretive society, with special ceremonies, which provided benefits to its members.

Liberal and Nationalist ideas were spread through a number of secret societies. These adopted the practices of the **freemasons**, with elaborate rituals, passwords, coded messages and special handshakes. Because of the secrecy surrounding these organisations, it is difficult to estimate the numbers involved, but they were probably small. Membership seems to have been mainly middle class, although they did attract a few nobles with liberal ideas. They had scarcely any working class or peasant following, however.

In the north were the Federati and the Adelfi. In the Papal States were the Spillo Negro ('Black Pin'), the Latinisti and the Bersaglieri. The best known group, however, was the Carbonari. This organisation was quite strong in the south, where it represented around 5% of the adult male population of Naples. It also spread to the Papal States and Piedmont-Sardinia, but was never as powerful in these areas. There was little co-ordination between the groups, scattered as they were in different parts of Italy, and their aims were never clearly defined. Although there was talk of the overthrow of the restored Italian rulers and the expulsion of Austria from Italy, most members seemed to have had more limited aims. They hoped for little more than the establishment of constitutional monarchies within the various states and, in general, seemed happier discussing what they were against, rather than what they were for.

1. Why was Italy divided into a number of separate states in 1815?

2. Who suffered most from this arrangement? Explain your answer.

3. Make a list of the factors that were (a) preventing and (b) encouraging political change in Italy after 1815. Which do you consider were the most influential? Give reasons for your answer.

The main rulers of Italy, 1815–1848

Kingdom of the Two Sicilies
House of Bourbon
Kings:
Ferdinand I 1759/re-established
1816–1825
Francis I 1825–1830
Ferdinand II 1830–1859

Kingdom of Piedmont-Sardinia
House of Savoy
Kings:
Victor Emmanuel
Charles Felix 1821–1831
Charles Albert 1831–1849

Grand Duchy of Tuscany
House of Habsburg
Dukes:
Ferdinand III 1814–1824
Leopold II 1824–1859

Duchy of Modena
House of Habsburg
Dukes:
Francis IV 1814–1846
Francis V 1846–1860

Duchy of Parma
House of Habsburg
Duchess:
Marie-Louise 1814–1847
House of Bourbon
Duke:
Charles II 1847–1849 (formerly
Duke of Lucca)

Duchy of Lucca
House of Bourbon
Duchess:
Maria Luisa 1817–1824
Duke:
Charles Ludwig 1824–1847
(Charles became Duke of Parma in
1847 and Lucca became part of
the Grand Duchy of Tuscany)

Papal States
Pope:
Pius VII 1800–1823
Leo XII 1823–1829
Pius VIII 1829–1830
Gregory XVI 1831–1846
Pius IX 1846–1878

Lombardy and Venetia
Directly ruled by Austrian Emperor
from 1814
House of Habsburg
Emperor:
Francis I 1804–1835
Ferdinand I 1835–1848

2.2 What were the causes and results of the revolutions of 1820–1821?

How did resistance develop 1815–1820?

Opposition to the 1815 settlement was mainly a secretive, underground movement between 1815 and 1820. With the restrictions that were in place on freedom of discussion and of the press, it was very hard for would-be revolutionaries to spread and co-ordinate the discontent. There were sporadic troubles like, for example, a rising at Macerata in the Papal States in 1817. However, disturbances were rarely well planned enough to escape detection and repression by the diligent secret police. Punishments for subversive activities could be severe. In the Papal States there was an endless struggle between liberal secret societies and the *Sanfedisti*, who supported the Pope. However, with the Pope's blessing, Cardinal Rivarola rooted out the troublemakers, condemned hundreds to exile or 'forced work' schemes and placed many more under police surveillance. He imposed compulsory monthly confession and annual attendance at a chosen **retreat**.

In two states, however, the troubles did pose a real threat to the rulers in the 1820s. These were the Kingdom of the Two Sicilies and the Kingdom of Piedmont-Sardinia.

Why was there an outbreak of revolution in the Kingdom of the Two Sicilies in 1820?

There were two strands to the opposition to Ferdinand's rule in the south. The Carbonari hated the influence of Austria and Ferdinand's autocratic style of government. The Sicilians resented their union with the mainland and felt, with some justification, that little attention had been paid to their

Sanfedisti: The 'Holy Faithful' was a society set up in opposition to the Carbonari. Members took an oath to 'show no pity for the wailing of children or the old, and to spill the blood of the infamous liberals to the last drop, regardless of sex or rank'.

Retreat: To go into retreat was a Catholic practice involving a period of quiet meditation and prayer at a holy place, such as a monastery.

The arrest of four members of the Carbonari in 1821.

What does this picture tell you about membership of the Carbonari?

needs since 1815. A fall in agricultural prices had hit the Sicilian peasants particularly badly and the departure of the court from Palermo to Naples had also caused unemployment in that city.

In 1817, the Austrian garrisons had been withdrawn from Naples and the maintenance of law and order was entrusted to a militia of volunteers under local officers. Unfortunately for the rulers, however, some of these militia were among those most hostile to Ferdinand's style of government. News of revolution in Spain encouraged the dissatisfied, who had long nurtured hopes of changing the regime and the Carbonari led a series of riots and demonstrations.

Ferdinand I's government made a few arrests, but these only fuelled the discontent. In July 1820, the garrison at Nola, a few miles east of Naples, broke into revolt. General Guglielmo Pepe, one of a number of officers made responsible for organising the new militia system, assumed control of the 'revolution'. He extended his forces by enrolling members of the Carbonari, even though he was not a member himself. When he led one infantry and two cavalry units in a march on Naples, the terrified King took to his bed.

How successful was the revolution?

At first, the 'revolution' looked as though it would easily succeed. King Ferdinand I promised freedom of the press and a constitution based on that granted to Spain in 1812. This was very liberal. It involved the abolition of the special privileges of the nobility and clergy, the destruction of the power of the Inquisition, and an elected parliament with a vote for all adult males. Ferdinand even took an elaborate oath to honour his word. 'Omnipotent God – if I do lie, do thou at this moment annihilate me.' Since the all-powerful Lord did not strike him down, his superstitious subjects were foolish enough to believe his promises.

Ferdinand's actions also encouraged further troubles in Sicily. Here, the revolution was led by the trade guilds, the Maestranze, who wanted the separation of Sicily from Naples. The Neapolitan Governor was forced to flee, as riots broke out in Palermo. Government offices were burned down and prisoners released from gaols, amidst demands for a separate Sicilian constitution.

The new Neapolitan Parliament, which met in Naples in October 1820, was made up of professional middle-class men, a few noblemen and priests. The King swore to defend the new constitution and Pepe was put in charge of the army. There was talk of the redistribution of land to the peasants and a reform of the Church. The parliament had no sympathy, however, for the Sicilian revolt and voted to send troops to restore Neapolitan domination.

Why did the revolution fail?

The Naples revolution was clearly a middle-class affair. Although the peasants provided a strong following in Sicily, the mainland leaders had no intention of including the lower classes in their new system of government. Although events had certainly frightened the ruler, Ferdinand I, and the other powers of Europe, the division of the revolt, the lack of popular support and the limited political experience of its leaders, meant that it soon collapsed. Metternich easily won Russia and Prussia over to his way of thinking at the **Troppau** Congress (October 1820), when he voiced his belief that revolution in one country could have an unsettling effect upon others and should therefore be put down.

In January 1821, Metternich invited Ferdinand to attend another congress, in **Laibach**, to discuss the developments in his kingdom.

Troppau/Laibach Congresses: At the Troppau Congress, the Troppau Protocol agreed on the principle of intervention against revolutions within states. The second congress (at Laibach) was a continuation of the first, at which it was resolved to put this principle into action in Naples.

Ferdinand was granted permission from his new Parliament to attend. They believed naively that he was going to gain international recognition for their new constitution – 'the sanction of the powers for our newly acquired liberties', as they put it. Instead, he sought Austrian support to restore his former powers. Once the Austrian army marched south, the revolution was fated. Despite an attempt at resistance from Pepe and his men, the rebels were defeated at Rieti on 7 March 1821. By 24 March, Austrian troops occupied Naples and the old regime was restored.

What was the result of the revolution in Piedmont-Sardinia in 1821?

News of the revolution in Naples had encouraged the secret societies of the north, who hoped to force Victor Emmanuel I to grant a constitution. Membership rose markedly in 1820–21 and there were a number of incidents. The first, a 'sit-in' of students at the University of Turin in January 1821, followed the pattern of earlier troubles and was violently broken up by the police. However, in March, events took a more serious turn. Undaunted by the depressing news from Naples, a group of aristocratic army officers, led by Count Santorre di Santarosa, showed their determination to press for change in Piedmont-Sardinia. Joined by a few liberal nobles, and a larger body of middle-class liberal revolutionaries, they took over the fortress of Alessandria. They set up a revolutionary government, proclaimed an independent 'Kingdom of Italy', and declared war against Austria.

Once again, despite their relatively small numbers, the revolutionaries had managed to strike fear into their ruler. Following another army mutiny in Vercelli, near Turin, Victor Emmanuel I chose to abdicate in favour of his brother, Charles Felix. He preferred this course of action to that of meeting the liberal demands for a constitution and of war against Austria.

Since Charles Felix was on a visit to Modena at this time, Charles Albert, the King's nephew, was made regent. Under pressure from the liberals, he issued a vague proclamation referring to the Spanish Constitution of 1812 as 'a law of the State'. The liberals believed they had triumphed, but Charles Albert's announcement was, of course, subject to the approval of Charles Felix.

Why did the revolution fail?

The return of Charles Felix brought the collapse of the liberal hopes. Having declared Charles Albert a rebel and exiled him to Tuscany, Charles Felix appealed to Metternich for military aid. Knowing he had the full support of his Holy Alliance allies, Metternich was not afraid to send Austrian troops to restore order. They joined forces loyal to Charles Felix and crushed the revolutionary armies at Novara, on the route from Milan to Turin, on 8 April 1821. By September, Charles Felix was in full possession of his kingdom.

What was the result of the failure of the revolutions of 1820–1821?

In the Kingdom of the Two Sicilies, the reprisals on those who had supported the revolution were swift and harsh. Pepe escaped to London and many fled the country or were exiled. Imprisonment, flogging, hanging and executions ensured there was no further trouble. Indeed, the reprisals were so severe that even Metternich intervened and sacked the Chief of Police.

In Piedmont-Sardinia, too, rebel leaders and thousands of revolutionaries were forced to flee abroad or risk harsh punishment. Many found

1. Where and why did revolution break out in Italy in 1820–1821?

2. Why did the revolutions fail? Give reasons to support your answer.

3. Metternich described the troubles in Italy in 1820–1821 as 'earthquakes' and 'torrents'. Do you think he was correct? Explain your answer.

themselves transported to Austrian prisons, although in contrast with the south, there were only two executions. The Austrians remained in Piedmont-Sardinia, with a 12,000-strong occupying army, until 1823, to prevent any further recurrence of trouble.

All over Italy, and even in areas such as Lombardy and the Papal States where there had been no revolution, liberals were hunted down and heavy sentences passed. It is estimated that around 2,000 were forced to leave the peninsula at this time. The experiences of 1820–21 made liberalism appear a lost cause in Italy.

2.3 Why, and with what results, was there further unrest in Italy in 1831?

Although it became even more difficult to organise political opposition within Italy after 1821, those committed to change continued to scheme from abroad, particularly from Paris and London. The outbreak of liberal revolution in France, in July 1830, raised hopes once more. It seemed that the French might be willing to support revolutions elsewhere, and this inspired unrest in Modena, Parma and the Papal States.

How were the disturbances in Modena and Parma similar to those of 1820–1821?

The disturbances in Modena and Parma followed a similar pattern to those of earlier years. They were led by the middle classes. In Modena, it was Enrico Misley, son of a university professor and a practising lawyer, who inspired the troubles. In nearby Parma, it was students who began rioting. The aim – constitutional reform – was also similar, although Misley took this a little further, with plans for the establishment of a central Italian Kingdom under Duke Francis IV of Modena.

Even the duplicity of a ruler who appeared to support the liberals' aims, but then took action against them, mirrored the events of Naples in 1821. Although Duke Francis IV was not a liberal, he was pompous enough to show an interest in Misley's plans and to receive Camillo Manzini, a condemned revolutionary who had managed to escape to London. Duke Francis IV waited until two days before the 'revolution' was due to be launched and, in February 1831, had its leaders arrested. Misley's supporters were limited in number and, had Francis IV not made the mistake of travelling to Vienna to seek Austrian support, the revolution would probably have collapsed.

The liberals once again enjoyed a brief moment of glory, as their rulers panicked. Duchess Marie-Louise of Parma followed Francis IV and provisional governments were established in the two states. However, events followed a familiar pattern and, although they set up a joint army to protect their fragile regimes, they had little time to prepare before Duke Francis IV returned, with Austrian support, to defeat them in March.

The disturbances had proved fruitless. The old rulers were restored. The Duke denied any sympathy and resumed his role as absolute monarch, exacting vengeance on those implicated in the troubles.

What was the result of the disturbances in the Papal States?

It was again the middle-class professionals who led the protests in the Papal States, and in particular in the Papal Legations (Bologna, Ferrara and Ravenna), who resented their loss of independence in 1815. The protests were similar to those elsewhere, although here the issue of Church domination of government was the major complaint. Early success led to the establishment of 'The Government of the Italian Provinces, in Bologna in February 1831, which deposed the Pope as ruler. However, the expected support from neighbouring states and from the French did not materialise. Without this, the provisional liberal government had little hope of surviving.

The disturbances in the Papal States demonstrated to would-be revolutionaries that France was to be of little help to them. Louis-Philippe had refrained from supporting the rebels in Modena, which was regarded as being within Austria's sphere of influence, but he might have been expected to intervene in Bologna, which was part of Papal territory. However, he was cautious, and the French Foreign Minister declared, 'the blood of Frenchmen belongs to France alone'.

When Austrian troops went to the Pope's aid and took Bologna on 21 March, Louis-Philippe declared that, if the Pope were to carry through some governmental reform, the French would support him. A five-power conference of ambassadors met in Rome, in May, and drew up a reform programme, which included the secularisation of the administration. When the Austrian army withdrew on 17 July, it looked as though the trouble was over. The Pope was restored, but with promises of reform.

However, the liberals had again been too easily appeased. The agreed changes were not fully carried out, but attempted uprisings were fruitless. The Austrian forces returned in January 1832 and occupied Bologna. France, who was not prepared to let Austria have a completely free hand, responded with the occupation of Ancona in January 1832, but this did little for the liberal cause. Although France remained in occupation of Ancona until 1838, Pope Gregory XVI, who was elected at the height of the crisis, relied on Austrian support. Papal administration, with all its faults, continued.

Why did the revolutions of the 1820s and of the 1830s fail?

The revolutions and disturbances of the 1820s and of the 1830s had much in common. Their failure can be attributed to a number of shared factors.

- The revolutions were all localised. In each case, local grievances or plans were the foremost concerns. Communication and co-operation were limited. The revolutionaries in Bologna, for example, refused to deplete their resources by sending help to Modena in 1831.

- The revolutions were led by the middle classes, who were not naturally inclined to violence. Most had fairly moderate aims and were easily satisfied, and even tricked, by their rulers.

- None of the revolutions, with the exception of that in Sicily, gained much support from the workers or peasants. The middle-class leaders did not even seek it. They would have been horrified by the prospect of the 'ordinary' people playing a part in government. When rulers fled, it was usually out of panic rather than because of the strength of the revolutionaries. The peasants did not understand the demands being made anyway and most were happy to cheer the returning rulers once the troubles were over.

- The revolutionaries were often ill-equipped. Even when army officers or militiamen were involved, their equipment could not match that of the professional armies of the Austrians. Those fighting in the Papal States, for example, carried little more than hunting guns, pikes and scythes.

- The failure of the French to intervene on the side of the revolutionaries after 1830 also allowed the absolutist regimes to survive. In both 1820–21 and 1830–31, there was no outside power prepared to intervene on the liberals' behalf.

● The revolutions were defeated by the power of Austria. Once assured of support at Troppau, Austria showed no hesitation in using its army to support the rulers. By 1831, five of the six main rulers in Italy (Piedmont-Sardinia was the exception) had called in Austrian troops to help them.

How far had Italy changed by 1831?

Italy, in 1831, was much like Italy in 1815. None of the revolutions had been successful and in the Kingdom of Piedmont-Sardinia, Naples and the Papal States, the traditional rulers were actually stronger than they had been before the revolutions. Sicily had been placed firmly under the grip of Naples. The trade guilds, that had been at the forefront of the troubles of 1821, had been abolished. Autocracy was re-established everywhere and those who had dared to challenge their states were either in prison or in exile.

However, there had been some changes.

● There were a number of new rulers. (See the table of Italian rulers on page 22.) Ferdinand I of Naples died in 1825, and was succeeded by his son, Francis I (1825–1830) and then his grandson, Ferdinand II (1830–1859). There was also a new Pope, Gregory XVI, who ruled from 1831 to 1846. There was a new King in Piedmont-Sardinia when Charles Albert, who had given hope to the rebels of 1821, came to power (1824–1849). All of these men were less marked by the conservative attitudes that had accompanied the rulers of the immediate post-1815 period. While they were not excessively 'liberal', they were nevertheless more receptive to ideas of change.

● By 1831, the great powers of Europe were no longer as unanimous about the need to keep things as they had been in 1815. Although Prussia and Russia had declared their support for Austria and for a policy of intervention against revolution in 1821, their interest in Italian affairs waned over the following years. Prussia had problems of its own in Germany, and Russia, in Poland. Britain and France had never supported the Troppau agreement anyway, and the troubles in Greece weakened the Austro–Russian alliance, while the revival of French power in Europe acted as a check on Austrian influence.

● The failure of the old-style secret societies, such as the Carbonari and Federati, meant that a new style of revolutionary politics was able to attract support. The chief protagonist of the new thinking was Giuseppe Mazzini.

1. In what respects were the revolutions of 1831 similar to those of 1821?

2. How important was the part played by foreign countries in the disturbances in Italy 1820–1831?

3. Which of the various revolutions of the period 1820–1831 do you think came nearest to success? Give reasons for your answer.

2.4 What was the contribution of Mazzini to the movement for change in Italy after 1831?

What were Mazzini's ideas?

The new 'Young Italy' society, launched by the 26—year-old Giuseppe Mazzini in Marseilles in 1831, was based on Mazzini's own views of how revolution was to succeed in Italy.

Mazzini believed that the aims of earlier revolutionaries – constitutional monarchy within the various states – were too moderate. He argued that true liberty would only be possible when Italy was united as a single nation. His society was, therefore, committed to nationalism – 'the universality of citizens speaking the same tongue', as he put it.

The methods of the early revolutionaries were also criticised. Mazzini believed they had been insufficiently committed and had expected countries, such as France, to do their work for them. Mazzini called on the Italian people and, in particular, the young people, to prove themselves worthy of their destiny, to educate themselves and to fight.

He also believed in a republican form of government. The new Italy was to be ruled by a central government, democratically elected. Members of his society took an oath to devote themselves to the creation of a 'free independent republican nation'.

How did 'Young Italy' differ from earlier revolutionary societies?

In some ways Mazzini's new society looked like those of the past. It had the old-fashioned ritual of secret passwords and handshakes. It was also supported by the educated middle classes and was never very successful with the peasantry. However, there were differences.

- 'Young Italy' was a youth movement. The upper age limit was 40 (later raised), but most members were much younger. Their motto was 'thought and action'. They wore a uniform of the national colours – green shirt, red belt, white trousers and a beret. They equipped themselves with weapons – a rifle and 50 rounds of ammunition per member.

- 'Young Italy' was not a localised affair. Its aims were for the whole of Italy, and its contacts international. Mazzini had grand plans for liberal change throughout Europe, and soon groups such as 'Young Germany', 'Young Ireland' and 'Young Europe' followed similar patterns.

How successful was Mazzini as a revolutionary?

In practical terms, Mazzini was spectacularly unsuccessful. Although a convinced republican, he wrote to Charles Albert, the new King of Piedmont-Sardinia, in 1824, asking him to 'Put yourself at the head of the nation; write on your banner "Union Liberty and Independence"'. The gesture achieved nothing, except possibly to encourage the severity with which the King crushed Mazzini's attempts to encourage a mutiny in the Piedmontese army in 1833.

Mazzini's attempt to invade Savoy from Switzerland in 1834 was a fiasco. The Genoan general placed in charge proved incompetent. He

---

Giuseppe Mazzini (1805–1872)

Son of a doctor from Genoa, he was highly intelligent and joined the Carbonari in 1827. He was arrested in November 1830 and forced into exile. He settled in Marseilles in France and, despairing of the unsuccessful conspiracies of the Carbonari, founded his own movement, 'Young Italy', in March 1831. Mazzini was a republican and spread a nationalist message. He hoped to increase patriotism so that Italians could expel the Austrians and bring about the unification of Italy. Although his planned risings were unsuccessful, he provided an inspiration to nationalists everywhere. Mazzini was a romantic figure. He always dressed in black, in mourning for Italy, and lived in rooms full of cigar smoke and canaries. He was forced to direct his movement in exile, firstly from Marseilles, and later from London (after 1837). Here, he amalgamated 'Young Italy' with similar movements abroad and created 'Young Europe'. He kept up a constant stream of letters and writings. Works such as *Duties of Man* and *Thoughts upon Democracy* were enthusiastically received in European radical circles and Mazzini's name became well known to the literate and politically aware classes of Italy. In 1848, he returned briefly to liberate Milan.

squandered the funds given to him to raise an army, allowed his Polish and German volunteers to be seized by the Swiss authorities, and lost the rest of his men while disagreeing with Mazzini over tactics.

There were many bungled attempts at insurrection. Giuseppe Garibaldi, who later became one of the leaders of Italian unification, was condemned to death for his part in the failed Mazzinian conspiracy in Genoa, although he managed to escape. In 1844 the Bandiera brothers, Emilio and Attilo, inspired by Mazzini's ideas, although against his advice, tried to raise a revolution in Naples. They sailed from Venice to the coast of Naples with 19 followers, but were attacked by the local peasants and townspeople. They were captured and nine of them, including the two brothers, were shot.

The martyrdom of the Bandiera brothers is a sign of one of the greatest weaknesses of 'Young Italy'. It never managed to appeal to the peasantry, and never attracted very large numbers. Mazzini estimated its following at about 50,000 at its greatest extent, but it is likely that he exaggerated. Furthermore, it was difficult for him to remain in control, when he spent his life in exile. Mazzini had been banished from France and Switzerland by 1837 and had to live in London until 1848.

What was Mazzini's contribution to the Italian cause?

Although Mazzini's conspiracies all ended in failure, he was very successful as a publiciser of ideas. He wrote thousands of letters and endless articles, which were smuggled into Italy and appeared in his society's newspapers and elsewhere. According to the historian Denis Mack Smith, Mazzini succeeded in 'defining the goal and arousing enthusiasm among practised soldiers and statesmen'. He is therefore important, not so much for what he did, but for the way he inspired many young radicals in this period. He gave their liberalism a new fervour and optimism which kept the cause alive in the face of adverse circumstances.

> **Giuseppe Garibaldi (1807–1882)**
> Son of a fisherman from Nice (Nizza), part of the kingdom of Piedmont-Sardinia. At 15, he ran away to sea and joined Mazzini's 'Young Italy' movement. Garibaldi was sentenced to death for taking part in Mazzini's planned invasion of Piedmont-Sardinia in 1833, but escaped to South America where he spent many years of exile. He fought in the civil wars in Argentina and gained a reputation as a guerrilla leader. He returned home in 1848 and devoted himself to the nationalist cause.

> 'Mazzini's ideas and inspiration transformed attitudes to change in Italy in the 1830s.' Do you agree or disagree with this statement? Give reasons for your answer.

2.5 What influences were promoting nationalism in Italy, 1831–1846?

What were the cultural influences?

In the 1830s and 1840s a new form of literature also began to rouse nationalist ideas. Romantic novels, such as *I Promessi Sposi* ('The Betrothed') by Alessandro Manzoni (published in Milan 1825–27), were popular among the reading classes. Based on past glories, they encouraged patriotic feeling. The arts were frequently used to deliver an anti-Austrian message. To avoid censorship, they would portray another foreign nation as the wicked oppressor. When 'John of Procida' by Giovanni Niccolini was performed in Florence in front of the French Minister, he was annoyed when the audience cheered the lines directed against the French. However the Austrian Minister sitting next to him is said to have observed, 'Don't take it badly. The envelope is addressed to you but the contents are for me!'

Even music was used as a vehicle for patriotic themes, as in Gioacchino Rossini's 'William Tell' and the early Giuseppe Verdi opera, 'The Lombards of the First Crusade'. Verdi was a close friend of Manzoni and he went on to compose many operas with similar themes, again using stories from other countries, such as 'Nabucco' and 'Macbeth', to evade censorship. Painters, too, depicted great battles, while poets such as Giacomo Leopardi glorified liberty.

What was the influence of the Riformisti?

Although, politically, Italy appeared to be standing still, there was a growing interest in social and economic reform after 1830. The *Riformisti* ('the reformers') was the name given to those who believed that economic reform was the key to Italy's future. They believed that, freed from Austria's restrictive influence, Italy could flourish again.

Their ideas were spread in journals, such as Gian Domenico Romagnosi's *Gli Annali* ('The Annals'), produced in Lombardy in the early 1830s, and Carlo Cattaneo's *Politecnico*. These stressed the importance of industrial growth to the future of Italy and put forward plans for savings banks, schools, and a common monetary system which would encompass several states. Scientific congresses, agricultural societies and the construction of the first railway in Italy (in Naples), in 1839, all helped to spread the progressive message. The cheese industry at Gorgonzola and the Chianti wine industry were examples of this concern for economic growth, and a belief that the future of Italy depended on its economic development.

The *Riformisti* opposed the republican, conspiratorial ideas of Mazzini and wanted co-operation between rulers and people in some sort of Italian federation. There was, however, a contradiction in their views. Many of their schemes, such as those for railways and banks, would cut across state boundaries and would inevitably undermine the power of individual rulers.

What were the ideas of the Albertisti?

As Charles Albert showed a greater willingness to reform in the 1830s, a 'monarchist' group, sometimes known as the *Albertisti*, developed. The Piedmontese part of Piedmont-Sardinia was the most economically developed part of Italy. From 1837, Charles Albert introduced extensive legal, administrative, financial and military reforms in his Kingdom. Commerce was encouraged with a reduction in tariffs, the University of Turin was expanded, and extensive plans for the development of railways were drawn up. This made Piedmont-Sardinia the only state capable of leading a national crusade against the Austrians, and some monarchists adopted the idea of Charles Albert as a future King of Italy.

The idea of the supremacy of Piedmont-Sardinia was reinforced by some of the political writings of the 1840s. Cesare Balbo wrote *Delle Speranze d'Italia* ('The Hopes of Italy') in 1844. He favoured a federal Italy under Charles Albert's leadership. Massimo D'Azeglio wrote *Degli Ultimi Casi di Romagna* ('Of the recent events in the Romagna') in 1846. He argued that the recent events in the chaotic Papal States proved that leadership in Italy would have to be granted to Charles Albert.

Most of Charles Albert's supporters favoured a north Italian kingdom, complete with a constitutional government and freedom of the press. However, no specific plans were put forward as to how this might be carried out, and the attitude of Charles Albert himself remained ambiguous. Historian Derek Beales refers to him as an opportunist who was merely interested in increasing the power of Piedmont-Sardinia. However, Charles Albert told D'Azeglio in 1845, 'at present there is nothing to be done, but rest assured that when the opportunity comes, my life, the life of my sons, my treasure and my army will all be spent in the cause of Italy'.

What other political views developed after 1831?

Outside Piedmont-Sardinia, Charles Albert was a less popular choice to lead a national revival, but the political writers everywhere shared a single belief. They paid no heed to the idea of a popular revolution, or democracy. Federalism was often seen as the best way forward. In Lombardy, for example, the writer Carlo Cattaneo's ideas were welcomed by the middle classes. He favoured an independent Lombard Republic that would eventually become a member of a federal republican Italian state. He argued that 'Italy is physically and historically federalist' and had too many differences in its laws, languages and customs for a united Italy to be successful.

Another influential writer was Abbé Gioberti, an exiled Piedmontese theologian and philosopher who wrote *Del Primato Morale e Civile degli Italiani* ('Of The Moral and Civil Primacy of the Italians'), popularly known as *The Primato,* in 1843. He believed that the Pope and the Catholic Church should lead the Italian national revival. Gioberti favoured a federation of states aided by a 'cabinet' of ruling princes, with the Pope as president. He made no specific mention of the expulsion of Austria, and condemned revolutionary means to unity. Although Gioberti's works attracted a fair amount of support, the reputation of the Papal States and Church as reactionary and oppressive stood in the way of his ideas.

How did economic and social developments affect Italy by the 1840s?

Throughout the first half of the 19th century, Italy's economy continued to be based on agriculture. However, Italian farming was inefficient, and vulnerable to foreign competition. This meant that the peasantry was badly affected by the long agricultural crisis, which began in the 1820s and reached its peak in the 1840s. Although the political ideas of the liberal reformers had little appeal for this class, their depressed condition nevertheless encouraged them to participate in acts of disorder, riot and arson. Agricultural prices were subject to fluctuations and this affected the town dwellers too. There were a number of city riots caused by the price of foodstuffs in the 1840s.

Italy had begun to move forwards economically in this period, but industrial development was largely confined to the north, where it inspired the *Riformisti.* Furthermore, economic growth had its downside. Workers in cities such as Milan and Turin, which had expanded rapidly in the first half of the 19th century, suffered from overcrowding, poor housing and intolerable working conditions. Elsewhere, towns were often decaying economically, and the populations of Venice and Palermo had fallen since 1815. Living standards in towns declined after 1810 and urban sanitary conditions in Italy were some of the worst in Europe. In Naples in the 1840s, life expectancy was just 24 years.

1. In what ways, and to what extent, did literature and the arts spread new ideas in Italy in this period?

2. In what ways were the different schemes for liberal and nationalist change in Italy after 1831 similar, and it what ways did they differ?

Source-based questions: Ideas for the future of Italy

SOURCE A

Aims: The independence of Italy, our Country. To give her a single government based on a constitution, freedom of the press and of worship, the same laws, currency and measures.
Methods: To spread liberal ideas and to communicate them to friends, by firmly convincing them of the unfortunate state of affairs of our Mother country. The press, gatherings and private conversations are opportune [suitable] means. Cunning and perseverance are needed, and, above all, the eradication [removal] of all kinds of prejudice.

From the aims of the Order of the Carbonari, the Italian secret society, which had branches in a number of States in the 1820s and 1830s.

SOURCE B

Young Italy is Republican and **Unitarian**.

Republican:
- because every nation is destined by the law of God and humanity to form a free and equal community of brothers, and the republican is the only form of government that ensures this future;
- because the monarchy necessarily involves the existence of an aristocracy, the source of inequality and corruption to the whole nation;
- because both history and the nature of things teach us that elective monarchy tends to generate **anarchy** and hereditary monarchy tends to generate **despotism**;
- because our Italian tradition is essentially republican; the whole history of our national progress is republican.

Unitarian:
- because without unity there is no true nation;
- because without unity there is no real strength and Italy, surrounded as she is by powerful, united and jealous nations, has need of strength before all things;
- because federalism would necessarily place her under the influence of one of the neighbouring nations;
- because by reviving local rivalries, it would throw Italy back on the middle ages.

Adapted from Mazzini's beliefs for 'Young Italy', the society he founded from Marseilles in 1831

SOURCE C

Italy has within herself all the conditions of her national and political *Risorgimento*, without internal upheavals or foreign invasions. Italian union cannot be obtained by revolutions. The principle source of Italian Union is the Pope who can unify the peninsula by means of a confederation of its princes. Federal government is natural to Italy and the most natural of all governments. The security and prosperity of Italy cannot be achieved otherwise than by an Italian alliance. Foreigners cannot prevent this alliance and far from opposing it they ought to desire it. Two provinces above all ought to co-operate to foster the opinion, which favours Italian unity, Rome and Piedmont.

Adapted from Gioberti's *The Primato*, an influential book of 1843

SOURCE D

The unitary solution is childish, no more than the fantasy of schoolboys. Confederations are the type of constitution most suited to Italy's nature and history. The only obstacle to confederation – a most serious obstacle – is foreign rule, which penetrates deep into the peninsula. An Italian confederation is neither desirable nor possible if a foreign power forms part of it. A democratic insurrection may continue for some time to be the hope of secret societies, but it cannot be an event to be reckoned on as part of any major undertaking.

From *The Hopes of Italy* by C. Balbo, the Piedmontese writer in 1844

---

1. Study Source D. Explain the reference to 'foreign rule which penetrates deep into the peninsula'.

2. In what respects do these four extracts agree with one another?

3. Study all of the sources. To what extent do Sources A and B differ from Sources C and D in their views of how Italy should be governed in the future?

4. Using the information given in this chapter and in these sources, why do you think that the views of the different societies and writers in Italy after 1821 had only a limited impact before 1846?

Unitarian: This refers to the creation of a single state (united or unified).

Anarchy: Without any organised authority. Anarchists regard all forms of government as oppressive.

Despotism: A despot is a monarch with absolute power who uses that power to oppress his/her people.

2.6 What was the effect of Pope Pius IX's election in 1846?

<table>
<tr>
<td>

Pius IX, Giovanni Mastai-Ferretti 1792–1878, Pope (1846–1878)

As a Cardinal, he had gained the reputation of being 'progressive'. He was a kind-hearted man who genuinely wished to improve conditions in the Papal States. He was never the 'liberal Pope' that some Italians, such as Gioberti, had believed on his election. Pius IX had no experience of politics and was surprised by the reaction to his liberalism. After the events of 1848, he adopted a far more traditional and conservative position.

</td>
<td>

When Pope Gregory XVI died, in June 1846, and Pius IX was elected, liberals everywhere grew hopeful. 'Pio Nono', as he became known, had a reputation for reforming ideas, and was familiar with Gioberti's writings. Furthermore, he began his **pontificate** by instituting a much-needed plan of reform in the Papal States. He appointed the liberal-minded Cardinal Gizzi as Secretary of State and issued a political amnesty allowing around 2,000 political prisoners, mainly ex-revolutionaries, to be released from gaol. He proposed legal and judicial reforms, and appointed commissions to investigate education and administration. He gave lay people a greater say in government and announced that gasworks and railways might be built in the Papal States, something that Gregory XVI had rigorously opposed. In 1847, he put forward the suggestion of an Italian customs union and he granted three major reforms:

</td>
</tr>
</table>

Pontificate: Period of time during which a pope is in power.

- freedom of the press

- setting up of a Consulta (an advisory body with laity among the elected representatives)

- appointment of a civic guard.

Although many of the Pope's plans were quite cautious, the liberals and radicals seized their chance. Freedom from censorship led to an outpouring of independent, free-thinking journals. Political clubs were set up throughout the Papal domains, and membership grew rapidly. The civic guard, intended to protect property and to curb violence, swiftly became an 'organisation of the people' and provided them with weapons.

There was excitement elsewhere too. In Venice, a speaker at the ninth congress of Italian scientists received rapturous applause every time he mentioned Pio Nono's name. The arrival of a new archbishop in the city of Milan provoked hymn singing to Pio Nono in the streets. Such was the popular hysteria that Metternich made it treason to shout 'Vivo Pio Nono' in Lombardy and Venetia. In the Kingdom of the Two Sicilies, King Ferdinand II also forbade cheers, and complained of 'the wretched little priest'.

Demands for reform elsewhere followed the Papal lead. Genoa sent a series of requests for change to the King in Piedmont. In October 1846, Charles Albert responded with a long list of reforming measures including freedom of the press. This enabled Italo Balbo and Camillo Cavour to found the newspaper *Il Risorgimento*. In Tuscany, Grand Duke Leopold II was forced to abolish the secret police and, in Lucca, a civic guard was formed.

Count Camillo Cavour (1810–1861)

Member of the Piedmontese aristocracy. After a brief spell in the army, he became interested in scientific farming. He visited Great Britain, where he made himself a fortune by farming using machinery and scientific methods on his family estates. He also showed an interest in the parliamentary system in Britain. Cavour invested in the developing industries of northern Italy, and did not begin an active political career until his late 30s when he founded, and became editor of, a new political journal, *Il Risorgimento*. This was first published in Turin in 1847 with the purpose of gaining support for a liberal, monarchical Italy. Cavour joined the Piedmontese parliament in 1850, and thereafter showed himself a capable politician, Prime Minister and one of the architects of Italian unification. Although sympathetic to liberal attitudes, he was more concerned to extend the power of Piedmont-Sardinia.

The agitation caused great alarm in the Austrian-controlled states. Metternich was to remark, 'we expected everything except a liberal Pope'. He quickly made treaties with Modena and Parma. In July 1847, he increased Austrian troops in Ferrara, which lay inside the Papal States, to protect the border with Lombardy. The action was a political error. It roused a storm of protests, uniting liberals and Papalists. The Pope appealed to the powers of Europe. Charles Albert offered to put the Piedmontese army at his disposal and began to talk of a war for the independence of Italy. In the face of all this, Metternich was forced to withdraw his garrisons, which added to Pius IX's reputation as a national hero.

Pope Pius IX had raised many hopes but, when his new Council finally met in October–November 1847, it was clear that he did not intend to go too far too quickly. He informed the new body that it would not 'detract minimally from the **sovereignty of the pontificate**'. Furthermore, although he might wish to see the Austrians driven out of Italy, as a Pope he could never be the one to declare war. In the event, that honour was left to Charles Albert.

On 3 January 1848, there were clashes in Lombardy between the people of Milan and the Austrian garrison stationed in the town. In Tuscany, after a long period of social unrest that had been building up since September 1847, there was a rising at Leghorn on 6 January. The troubles in Milan grew worse over the following weeks as the patriotic middle-class Italians staged tobacco strikes, symbolically giving up smoking to deprive the Austrians of the tobacco duty which they collected. The riots became serious, and an Austrian cavalry charge through the city killed several people.

Between 12 and 27 January, Palermo, in Sicily, rose in revolt and drove out the Neapolitan forces. The movement spread to the mainland. On 29 January, Ferdinand II granted a constitution. Piedmont-Sardinia and Tuscany followed suit in February and the Pope in March. The same month, Austrian troops were forced out of Milan and Venice after several days of street fighting. Charles Albert seized the lead, declaring war on the Austrians in March. It looked as though Italy's moment of glory had arrived but, within a year, those hopes had been shattered.

Sovereignty of the pontificate: The complete power of the Pope to rule his states as he saw fit.

1. Why did the election of Pope Pius IX cause such excitement in Italy?

2. What can you learn about these revolts from this illustration?

Rioting in Palermo in January 1848. Typical of many of the disturbances which took place in rural areas of Italy, 1815–1848.

2.7 How widespread was nationalism in Italy before 1848?
A CASE STUDY IN HISTORICAL INTERPRETATION

The historian H. Hearder, in *Italy in the Age of the Risorgimento* (1983), comments that 'history is to a great extent written by the victors'. He is referring to the tendency of Italian historians, writing after unification in 1861, to regard the events of the early 19th century as a natural prelude to *Il Risorgimento*, the 'national revival' and Italian unification.

Perhaps the most famous of this school of writing was the Italian, Benedetto Croce, who produced, among other books, *History as the Story of Liberty*. In the 1920s and 1930s, when the Fascists were in power in Italy, an emphasis on the 19th-century rebirth of Italy became even more fashionable. Fascist historians tried to glorify the role of Italian nationalism. They wrote of its power in encouraging the people to resist foreign oppression and in unifying their nation. Similarly, in the 20th century, Italian Socialist historians have glorified those who led the secret societies and the rebellions of the 1820s, 1830s and of 1848. English liberal historians, such as George Macaulay Trevelyan, writing at the beginning of the 20th century, also saw the history of Italy as part of the steady growth of liberalism and nationalism, with the rebels fighting the conservative prejudices of their oppressive rulers.

The case for

- The writings and cultural changes that were taking place in Italy in the first half of the century might be considered part of a national revival. Developments in literature, music, poetry and painting encouraged a feeling of unity, a pride in being Italian and an hostility to the idea of separate regional states.

- The cultural revival spread a national language and encouraged people to think of themselves as Italians. It helped to break down the regional barriers.

- Nationalism grew stronger in the face of foreign rule in Lombardy and Venetia, and oppression elsewhere. The attitudes of rulers encouraged the secret societies, rebellions and mutinies. Although these were unsuccessful, they helped to spread patriotism, and their martyrs helped to win more converts to the cause.

- Many, especially the young, were encouraged to take direct action as a result of the teachings of Mazzini, who specifically preached the nationalist message.

Consequently, it is argued, the constant unrest throughout Italy in the early 19th century gradually converted the masses to nationalism. By 1848, there were many prepared to fight for the Italian cause. Italian nationalism had become a popular movement and only needed leaders to carry it to success.

The case against

Historian Derek Beales, in *Risorgimento and the Unification of Italy* (1981), refers to the nationalist arguments as 'the patriotic myth'. Most modern historians, even in Italy, which became a republic after World War II, have questioned the romantic view of Italy's 'rebirth', with its idea of a gradual growth of nationalism after 1815. Denis Mack Smith, Hugh Seton-Watson and Derek Beales all favour the view that nationalism made little progress in Italy before 1848, and that Italy's eventual unification was quite a chancy affair. Without knowing what was to follow, they argue, the troubles in Italy prior to 1848 could easily have been dismissed as minor upsets with little long-term impact.

- Rebels were often uncertain in their aims and the revolts were certainly not all inspired by nationalist motives. Some merely sought constitutional or liberal concessions from rulers, while the Sicilians, for example, sought separation from mainland Italy.

- The rebellions failed, partly because of their localism and the lack of co-ordination and co-operation between the different groups and states. Traditions of local allegiance went deep. Some of the north Italian states, in particular, had a long history of self-government and some saw little point in expelling Austria, only to replace its domination with that of Piedmont-Sardinia. These were hardly nationalist attitudes.

- National unity was rarely considered before the 1840s, and was not the only view put forward for the future development of Italy even then. Federalism, which emphasised the 'separateness' of the different states, was considered an equal possibility.

- Nationalism never affected the mass of Italian people. The peasants were never much involved in the troubles. Only a small minority ever participated in the liberal movements before 1848 and, when they did rebel, it was usually for economic reasons. Barriers of dialect, custom, prejudice and the lack of a formal education system meant that the vast majority of Italians probably had little genuine understanding of what nationalism meant, or what inspired the revolutionaries' activities.

- The supporters of the unrest were drawn from a narrow circle of the middle classes, mainly professionals, intellectuals and army men who were joined by a few liberal aristocrats. They were also mainly from the north of Italy. It was this narrow group of people who were most affected by the cultural revival, but their actions must have owed at least as much to their desire for advancement as to their commitment to nationalism. They shunned the support of the illiterate peasantry, and concentrated on the type of political and economic reform that would most benefit their own type.

- Not until the 1840s did the Italians share a national language. French was the language of government in Piedmont-Sardinia and the 'Kingdom of the Two Sicilies', Latin in the Papal States, and German in the Austrian areas. Ordinary people used local dialects. Even Mazzini spoke a dialect as his first language, French as his second. Such divisions were bound to prevent the growth of nationalism.

- Membership of the Italian societies and involvement in rebellions was small. Garibaldi listed those who took part in the rising in Piedmont-Sardinia, in 1821, as 'in all six superior officers, 30 secondary officers, five physicians, 10 lawyers and one Prince'. The rebellions were too weak and badly organised to have much impact and may well have increased opposition to, rather than encouraged support for, nationalist change.

Historian Denis Mack Smith has made an intensive study of this period of Italian history. He points out that the areas where nationalism might have been expected to make the most headway – Lombardy and Venetia – were reasonably content and loyal, at least until 1840. In that year, the Milan Chamber of Commerce even voted in favour of joining the German *Zollverein*, so remote were its feelings from those of Italian nationalism. Although the Austrian taxation policy caused dissatisfaction, these areas were generally the most prosperous in Italy. What is more, censorship and police methods did not press unduly harshly. Massimo d'Azeglio was to write, in his *Recollections* (published in 1867), 'it was essential not to shout too loud, with prudence one could say anything'. Consequently, there was no nationalist upsurge in these areas before the 1840s.

Elsewhere too, historians have shown that the Italian rulers were not the oppressive autocrats that some liberal historians have made them out to be. Rulers, such as Charles Albert and Pope Pius IX, in particular, were willing and capable of transforming their states. Since Italy was making progress anyway, it is argued, nationalist ideas were not only confined to a minority they were also irrelevant.

---

1. What evidence suggests that nationalism was steadily growing in Italy from 1815 to 1848?

2. Why have historians disagreed over the extent of nationalism in Italy before 1848?

3. Using the evidence of this Chapter, to what extent do you feel that Nationalism had taken hold in Italy before 1848? Give reasons for your answer.

---

1. Which of the reasons in the mind map was the most important in explaining the failure of the revolutions in Italy in 1848–49? Explain your answer.

2. Can you find links between the reasons for failure mentioned in the mind map?

For instance, the creation of the Roman Republic and the intervention of France are linked. Can you find any other links?

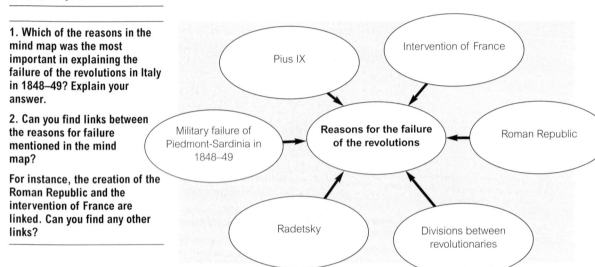

2.8 Why did Italian nationalists consider the prospects of Italian freedom and statehood so promising in 1846–1848?

The economic and political state of Italy: the beginnings of conservative reform?

If the initial outbreak of violence in France came as a surprise, the disturbances in Italy were wholly predictable. The political and economic crises in the Italian states had roots going back to the restoration of 1815 and, in many cases, far beyond. Economic hardship in Italy was the result, not merely of a temporary, cyclical crisis, but of long-standing backwardness.

Radical and nationalist politics also had a long history in Italy, yet there were some signs, in the years immediately before 1848, that the time might be ripe for change. Traditionally, Italy's political regimes have been portrayed as reactionary, out of date and as resistant to change as the Italian economy had been. While there is much evidence to support such an image, it is also possible that the years before 1848 witnessed changes that might have offered hope to more moderate Italian reformers. Recent research has suggested that some of Italy's conservative regimes were gradually coming to realise the advantages of modernisation and efficiency, as the mid-century approached. Metternich himself seems to have realised the advantages of combining legitimist principles with the greater efficiency that the Napoleonic administrations had achieved.

Vittorio Fossombroni in Tuscany and Luigi de Medici in Naples provide examples of ministers who attempted to implement such policies. Above all, a revisionist study by Narcisso Nada has emphasised the extent of the legal, administrative, financial and military reforms brought about by Charles Albert in Piedmont long before he placed himself at the head of the national cause. Seen in this light, 1848 does not represent a clean break with past Italian history, and the actions of both Charles Albert and Pope Pius IX may be seen as part of a longer process of 'conservative reform'. The reformist policies of Cavour may be seen to have had a much older pedigree.

For the churchman Vincenzo Gioberti, however, the future of Italy lay not with Piedmont, but with the Papacy. Gioberti, in his work *Of the Moral and Civil Primacy of the Italians* (*Del Primato Morale e Civile degli Italiani*), published in 1843, had portrayed the Papacy and the Catholic Church as the chosen agents of Italian national revival. He condemned revolutionary means towards unity, made no specific mention of the expulsion of the Austrians from the peninsula, and advocated a confederation of Italian states under the presidency of the Pope. The scheme certainly had the merits of preserving the local status of the individual princes and of placing the Austrians in the potentially embarrassing position of opposing the head of their own Church. On the other hand, up to 1846, there had seemed little prospect of finding a Pope willing to play the role designed for him by Gioberti and his **'neo-guelph'** supporters. Abruptly, however, in 1846, it seemed that Gioberti might have hit upon the right path.

The election of Pius IX

It is misleading to refer to the events in Italy as part of 'the revolutions of 1848' for that particular phase of Italian history began in 1846 with the sensational election of Cardinal Giovanni Mastai-Ferretti as Pope. Under his chosen title of 'Pius IX', he was one of the key figures in the events of the next two years.

The election of Pope Pius IX appeared to transform overnight the prospects of success for that form of federal unity envisaged by Gioberti and the neo-guelphs. In his initial burst of political reform Pius **amnestied** political prisoners and accepted a measure of non-clerical participation in government. In 1847 he put forward the suggestion of an Italian customs union. When Austria, thrown off balance by this 'liberal' Pope, dropped the broad hint of establishing a garrison at Ferrara (July 1847) within Papal territory, Pius protested so vigorously that he became a national hero for such an anti-Austrian gesture. For all his subsequent failure to lead the Italian cause to success, the election of Pius had a stimulating effect upon Italian politics. 'It must have seemed,' wrote the historian G. Berkeley, in *Italy in the Making, 1815–1848* (1940), 'as if the chief anti-nationalist stronghold of [the nationalists'] opponents had suddenly hoisted their own *tricolor*.'

Charles Albert and Piedmont

The second key figure of these years in Italy was Charles Albert, King of Piedmont since 1831. Italian nationalist historians in the intervening century have created a 'legend of Charles Albert', gallantly sacrificing his own interests, even his own throne, in the national cause. Today it is more acceptable to view him either as 'a romantic without the willpower to transform his vision into reality' (as did the Italian A. Omodeo) or like

'Neo-guelph': In medieval Italy the Guelph faction supported the political claims of the Papacy, as opposed to the Ghibelline faction, which favoured the rival claims of the Holy Roman Empire. Because Vincenzo Gioberti and his followers also placed the Pope in a position of political prominence, they were regarded as the 'new Guelphs'.

Amnestied: Granted official state pardons.

1. What did Italian nationalists
hope for in 1848 (a) from Pope
Pius IX and (b) from Charles
Albert of Piedmont-Sardinia?

2. How convincing is the
argument that events in Italy in
1848 owed more to traditional
Italian politics than to
revolutionary events elsewhere
in Europe?

Derek Beales, in *The Risorgimento and the Unification of Italy* (1981), as a
thorough conservative.

Certainly, Italian conservatism appeared to be in crisis even before the
rising in Paris. In January 1848, patriotic middle-class Italians staged a
'tobacco strike', giving up smoking in order to deprive the Austrians of the
revenue from their tobacco duty. On 12 January, Palermo, in Sicily, rose in
revolt against government from Naples. In February and March, the rash of
new constitutions began to affect Italy too. Tuscany received one from its
grand duke (11 February), and Naples from its king. Even the Pope could
not avoid the fashion (4 March). Also in March, Austrian troops were
expelled from Milan and Venice after several days of street fighting.
Charles Albert did not stop at the granting of a constitution. Less than
three weeks later, he committed Piedmont to war against the apparently
disintegrating Austrians, in support of the risings in Lombardy and
Venetia. With reluctant initial support from Naples and the Papacy,
Charles Albert had at least the superficial appearance of leading the
greatest bid in modern Italian history for freedom and nationhood.

2.9 How was Austria able to reassert its conservative influence over Italy?

The defeat of Piedmont

For all the theories and ideologies of the previous decades, the chance for
nationalist action in Italy had been provided by the disruption of the
European *status quo* and, especially, by the distraction of the Austrian
armed forces. The return of European stability, and the recovery of the
Austrian government spelled the doom of Italian freedom. A month after
the triumph of Windischgräätz in Prague, the Piedmontese army met the
forces of Marshal Radetzky at Custoza (25 July 1848). The Papacy and the
King of Naples had already withdrawn their troops, and defeat badly
undermined Piedmontese morale. Although the army survived largely
intact, the pessimism of the generals and Charles Albert's own fear of
radical activity at home led to retreat from Lombardy.

Renewed pressures upon the king only led to another defeat at Austrian
hands at Novara (23 March 1849). The price paid, this time, was the
permanent removal of Charles Albert from political life through his abdication in favour of his son, Victor Emmanuel. In addition, Austria imposed
an indemnity of 75 million lire upon Piedmont. That it retained its territorial integrity was due mainly to the European objections that would have
been raised to any tampering with this important 'buffer' zone on France's
borders. Charles Albert's proud boast that 'Italy will do it herself' (*Italia
fara da se*) had proved absolutely empty.

The flight of Pius IX

The war had also served to demonstrate the limitations of Pius IX as a
leader of the national cause. Leading a confederation of Italian states was
one thing. To lead one Catholic state against another was quite a different
matter. Pius' **confidant**, G. Montanelli, put the kindest interpretation upon
the Pope's motives. 'As an Italian he wanted to see the foreign invaders
driven out of the country, but as Pope – as the universal Father – he could
never declare a war of independence against Austria.' A more recent
historian, E.L. Woodward, has interpreted the whole pretence of liberal-
national leadership as a piece of confused thinking. 'How could the
Sovereign Pontiff become a constitutional ruler? Who could be responsible for the actions of the Vicar of God on earth?' Nevertheless, Pius

Confidant: A person with whom
people can discuss private problems
and other secret matters.

Sovereign Pontiff: A sovereign is the
person who is regarded as having the
highest level of authority; the Pontiff
is the Pope.

continued to work with his constitutional government until November. Then he fled Rome for the safety of Naples. With his flight, died the last hope of the Papacy fulfilling the role that Gioberti had mapped out for it.

The defeat of radicalism

'The royal war is over, the war of the people begins', declared Mazzini in a national appeal in August 1848. The flight of the Pope paved the way for a second, equally unsuccessful, phase in the struggles of 1848–49, the republican phase. In February 1849, a Roman Republic was proclaimed to fill the vacuum left by Pius. With Mazzini providing its political inspiration, and Giuseppe Garibaldi conducting its military defence, the Republic represented the pinnacle of radical aspirations. Its decrees, calling for the distribution of Church lands to the peasantry and for the public housing of the poor, could not offset its weaknesses. It was ravaged by inflation, starved of support from other quarters of Italy, and subjected to the combined hostility of France and Austria. After a heroic defence, the Republic was defeated, in June 1849, and the presence thereafter of a French garrison in Rome strengthened foreign interest in Italy's future.

Meanwhile, with the defeat of Piedmont, both Venice and Tuscany had gone their respective ways. Under the leadership of Daniele Manin, Venice once more declared itself a Republic, as it had been until the Napoleonic invasion. It resisted Austrian siege warfare, with its horrors of bombardment, cholera and starvation, until late August 1849. Tuscan radicals expelled their Grand Duke, in February 1849, but could not do the same to the Austrian forces that came to restore him in April.

The combination of circumstances in Italy in 1848–49 made those years seem particularly auspicious for the cause of Italian freedom. Yet what did it all achieve? Firstly, we find the famous judgement of G.M. Trevelyan that 1848 was 'the turning point at which modern history failed to turn'. Then we have the judgement of the patriot, Luigi Settembrini, that 'this generation made Italy', and that the example of 1848 was 'the point at which we became Italians, felt ourselves united and gathered together under a single standard'. We must conclude that, although the rebels of 1848 achieved nothing material in Italy, except for the Piedmontese constitution, the future course of Italian history was significantly altered. The refusal of Pius IX to put himself at the head of the national cause, and his conservative response to the events in Rome, killed the hopes of Gioberti and the neoguelphs.

The failure of radical republicanism demonstrated once more its various faults: the failure of its various advocates to co-operate with one another, and its impotence in the face of opposition from a major power. Leopold II, Grand Duke of Tuscany, and Ferdinand of Naples had shown their true colours by refusing to co-operate with Charles Albert, and much of northern Italy was more firmly than ever under the control of Austria.

The one exception to this catalogue of gloom was the state of Piedmont-Sardinia, whose king had embraced a constitution and staked his soldiers' lives and his own crown upon the Italian cause. Italian nationalists were not likely to forget those actions. The future of Italy, as the next two decades were to prove, lay with Piedmont-Sardinia.

1. What effect did the events of 1848–49 have on the political credibility of (a) the Papacy and (b) the Piedmontese monarchy?

2. To what extent is it true that the balance of power in Italian politics was the same after the revolutions of 1848–49 as it had been before?

Further Reading

Texts designed for AS and A2 Level students

The Unification of Italy by Andrina Stiles (Hodder & Stoughton, Access to History series, 1986)

Nationmaking in Nineteenth-Century Europe by W.G. Shreeves (Nelson, Advanced Studies in History, 1984)

More advanced reading

Risorgimento and the Unification of Italy by Derek Beales (Longman, 1981)

Risorgimento: The Making of Italy 1815–1879 by E. Holt (Macmillan, 1970)

The Making of Italy 1796–1870 by Denis Mack Smith (Macmillan, 1968)

Italy in the Age of the Risorgimento, 1790–1870 by Harry Hearder (Longman, History of Italy series, 1984)

The Risorgimento and the Unification of Italy by Derek Beales (Longman, 1981)

3 The unification of Italy

Key Issues

- What were the main obstacles to Italian unification in the 1850s and 1860s?

- Was the main aim of Piedmont to unify Italy, or merely to increase its own power?

- How important was foreign intervention in bringing about Italian unification?

3.1 What were the political priorities of the Kingdom of Piedmont-Sardinia in the early 1850s?

3.2 Why did Piedmont participate in the Crimean War and what did it achieve by its participation?

3.3 How was Piedmont able to launch a war against Austria in 1859?

3.4 How successful was the war of 1859 from the point of view of the Piedmontese government?

3.5 What were the political aims and methods of Giuseppe Garibaldi?

3.6 Historical interpretation: To what extent should Cavour be regarded as a champion of Italian unification?

3.7 What problems faced the new Italian state in the 1860s?

3.8 By what means, and with what success, did the Italian state extend its influence over other Italian territories?

Framework of Events

1850	Cavour appointed Piedmontese Minister for Trade, Agriculture and the Navy
	Passage of the Siccardi Laws
1851	Cavour appointed Prime Minister of Piedmont-Sardinia
1855	Piedmont joins Britain and France in the Crimean War
1856	Congress of Paris
1857	Foundation of the National Society
1858	January: Orsini's attempted assassination of Napoleon III
	July: Pact of Plombières between Cavour and Napoleon III
1859	April: Austrian declaration of war on Piedmont-Sardinia
	June: Battle of Magenta; Battle of Solferino
	July: Armistice signed at Villafranca
	November: Treaty of Zurich
1860	March: Plebiscites in Central Duchies in favour of unity with Piedmont
	May: Garibaldi's expedition to Sicily. Battle of Calatafimi
	September: Garibaldi's forces enter Naples
	October: Meeting between Garibaldi and Victor Emmanuel at Teano
1861	March: Victor Emmanuel II proclaimed King of Italy
	June: Death of Cavour
1862	Garibaldi's attempt to capture Rome defeated by Italian forces at Aspromonte
1866	June: Italian declaration of war against Austria. Italian defeat at Custoza
	July: Defeat of Italian navy at Lissa
	October: Union of Venetia with Italy
1867	Garibaldi's attempt to capture Rome
1870	September: Occupation of Rome by the Italian army. Rome incorporated in the Kingdom of Italy.

Overview

THE events of 1848–49 had an arguably greater impact upon Italian politics than upon the politics of any other part of western Europe. Yet the changes that they brought about were subtle, and may not have been immediately obvious to many contemporaries. No significant changes were made to the boundaries of the Italian states, and the balance of power between Austrian military strength and the forces of radical nationalism remained unchanged, with Austrian control firmly re-established. Indeed, with a French garrison now lodged in Rome the influence of foreign powers over Italian politics appeared to be stronger than ever.

Yet two important changes had taken place. One of the leading Italian states, Piedmont-Sardinia (which was in two parts – the state of Piedmont and the island of Sardinia – see map on page 50), had changed direction and had established an agenda that differed significantly from the usual reactionary stances of Italian rulers. Despite the efforts of two generations of Italian nationalist historians, few authorities seriously consider now that this agenda included the unification of Italy. Instead, King Victor Emmanuel II maintained his father's vision of a more powerful Piedmontese state, capable of dominating the richer, northern regions of Italy. Such a state would be enhanced and strengthened by the modern economic and political policies implemented by his leading minister, Camillo di Cavour. Taking his lead from the recent experiences of Britain and of France, Cavour belonged to a new generation of European conservatives who sought to harness industrial and commercial progress to maintain the political authority of the traditional governing classes. The other great change had not occurred in Italy, but it had profound political significance for the peninsula. The election of Louis Napoleon Bonaparte as President (later Emperor) of France brought to power a man with a vested interest in the revision of the European balance of power. Where, before 1848, the major powers had rigidly maintained the balance and the boundaries established by the Congress of Vienna, Napoleon III based his foreign policy on their readjustment and, in particular, on the reduction of Austrian power in central and southern Europe.

Thus, in the 1850s, there were four forces at large in Italian politics, as Piedmont-Sardinia interacted with the aspirations of nationalists and of the French Emperor against the power of Austria. The alliance between Piedmont-Sardinia and France appeared to offer the best prospect for change that Italy had known since the Napoleonic Wars, but it was not successful. At least, it did not achieve the results that Cavour had anticipated. It did not drive the Austrians out of northern Italy, and did not create the strong northern Italian state that Cavour desired. Nevertheless, it did transform the political balance of Italy. Shaken, if not shattered, Austrian power was in no position to offer its traditional protection to the conservative governments of central and southern Italy. Under these circumstances, Piedmont was able to take action in the **Central Duchies** which would never have succeeded before. Piedmontese ambitions did not extend to Naples or to Rome, but those regions were firmly on the agenda of Giuseppe Garibaldi and the '**party of action**'.

In general, in the course of the *Risorgimento*, the initiatives of the radical Italian nationalists were not remarkable for their timing. The great exception occurred in 1860, for Garibaldi's military expedition to Sicily (and subsequently to Naples) took

Central Duchies: The collective name given to the Duchies of Tuscany, Modena and Parma, lying just to the south of Piedmont.

'Party of Action': Term used to describe those radicals, such as Giuseppe Mazzini and Giuseppe Garibaldi, who hoped to bring about the unification of Italy by direct and popular military action.

place at exactly the right moment. By its timing, it was able to exploit Austria's military defeat, French war-weariness, and the uncertainty and vulnerability of the conservative Italian rulers. Garibaldi's actions forced Piedmont-Sardinia, facing a deadlock in the affairs of northern Italy, to turn its attention to the south. In the final twist of a highly pragmatic career, Cavour resolved to extend Piedmont-Sardinia's control over southern Italy in order to forestall the establishment there of a dangerous, radical regime. This was enormously successful in the short term, for Garibaldi chose to hand over his conquests to the King of Italy. In the longer term, however, Cavour's actions had consequences of even greater significance. Instead of consolidating its control over the prosperous north, as had been its main aim for more than a decade, Piedmont now stretched its resources in an attempt to control territories in the south, to which it had previously never aspired.

In effect, Garibaldi's achievement in 1860 was to wrest the initiative from Piedmont-Sardinia, to impose his programme of wider unification upon Cavour, and to hasten the creation of a unitary Italian state such as the radical nationalists had always envisaged. The Italian state that emerged from the 1850s and 1860s, therefore, was a hybrid that grew from the different aspirations of its different creators. Its constitutional nature was determined by the work of Cavour and of the Piedmontese monarchy, but its geographical extent in the end was largely determined by the programme of the radical nationalists.

1. Which of the individuals mentioned in the mind map was most responsible for Italian unification? Give reasons for your answer.

2. Which war was most important for creating a unified Italy? Explain your answer.

3. Can you identify any links between the points in the mind map in creating a unified Italy? For instance, the Pact of Plombieres, the Franco-Austrian War and Napoleon III are linked. Can you find any other links?

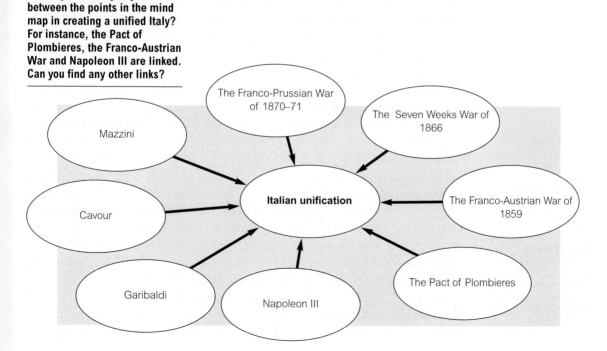

3.1 What were the political priorities of the Kingdom of Piedmont-Sardinia in the early 1850s?

Buffer state: A neutral state that lies between two other states, and serves to prevent their interests from clashing.

After the nationalist failures of 1848–49, Italy presented a sorry picture. Austria's military occupation was as strong as ever, political reaction was restored in the states of southern and central Italy, and most of the constitutions installed there had been suppressed. The **buffer state** of Piedmont, in the north-west corner of Italy, was the only exception to this rule. Although decisively defeated at Custoza and at Novara, it retained its constitution, the integrity of its territory and its freedom from Austrian occupation. On the face of it, these were encouraging signs for the moderate nationalists who now transferred their hopes from Pius IX to the Piedmontese monarchy. The ruler to whom Vincenzo Gioberti and others now looked, after the abdication of Charles Albert, was his son, the 29-year-old Victor Emmanuel II.

What was the political stance of Victor Emmanuel II?

The new king inherited not only his father's throne, but also the legend that Charles Albert had created by his actions in 1848–49. Victor Emmanuel's role, in the events of the next two decades, allowed later generations of Italian historians to create an even more compelling 'official' view of the king. In 1850, Victor Emmanuel was the saviour of Piedmont-Sardinia and of the Piedmontese constitution from the victorious Austrians, and his subsequent actions made him the champion of Italian constitutional monarchy, as well as the father of his country. Contemporary views of the King of Piedmont-Sardinia were often less spectacular. He was sufficiently ambiguous in his political views to be regarded as a cautious liberal by the British, and as a cautious conservative by the Austrians. He was probably just cautious. Contemporaries detected courage and good sense in him, but also found him lazy and coarse. Historian Denis Mack Smith concludes, in *Cavour* (1985), that the King was the sort of man 'always happiest in either the barracks, the stables or the hunting field'.

Victor Emmanuel's background contained little that was likely to make him a nationalist or a liberal. He was educated and trained to be heir to an autocracy, and his mother and wife were both members of the Austrian imperial family. Against claims that Victor Emmanuel bravely defended the Piedmontese constitution against the victorious Austrians, Denis Mack Smith points out that Austria had reasons of its own for favouring a compromise settlement. It was in the Austrian interest, too, that the Piedmontese monarchy should be strong enough to resist pressure from the radicals and, even more important, that Piedmont-Sardinia should have no cause to turn to France for assistance. Besides, the representative nature of the Piedmontese constitution (*il statuto*) should not be exaggerated. Of the two parliamentary chambers, the upper one was directly appointed by the king and, in the election of the lower house, the requirement that voters should be literate limited the electorate to only 2.25% of the population. Under the terms of the constitution, the king retained much personal power – the most important elements of which were command of the army and the power to appoint and dismiss his ministers at will.

The D'Azeglio ministry in Piedmont, 1849–1852

Victor Emmanuel's first domestic actions were not exactly those of a liberal. His first task was to ensure his control of the kingdom by means

Massimo D'Azeglio (1798–1866)
Entered politics after an early career as a landscape artist and an author of patriotic works. Saw action against Austria in 1848–49. Appointed Prime Minster of Piedmont (1849). Appointed Cavour to his cabinet, and lost office to him in 1852. Subsequently served as Piedmontese Commissioner in the Romagna (1859) and as governor of Milan (1860).

that included the shelling of Genoa to win it back from the radicals who remained entrenched there. His first administration included several of the 25 military men who were to hold ministerial office during his reign, although by the end of 1849 the administration was in the hands of a group of moderate conservatives under the leadership of Massimo D'Azeglio.

The first major policy of the ministry concerned one of the great liberal principles of the 19th century, the contest for power and influence between the Church and the State. Neither King nor Minister wished to tolerate the considerable influence of a body that had set its face so firmly against them both in 1848. The batch of measures, produced in 1850 and known as the Siccardi Laws, was a substantial first move in a decade of Piedmontese anti-clericalism. Church courts and other ecclesiastical privileges were abolished, the number of holy days was limited, and the senior Piedmontese churchman, Archbishop Fransoni, was imprisoned when he ordered his clergy to ignore these measures.

Such determined measures were rare from D'Azeglio. Having found a parliamentary majority hard to come by in the first place, he found it undermined, in 1852, by an opportunistic alliance between the leader of the 'middle-class party', Urbano Rattazzi, and his own Finance Minister, Camillo di Cavour. The fall of his ministry was assured when the King refused to accept the next stage of D'Azeglio's anti-clerical legislation, a bill enforcing civil marriage (May 1852). D'Azeglio was replaced by the most influential figure in the history of 19th-century Italy.

Cavour's desire for domestic political stability

Cavour's domestic administration of Piedmont, between 1852 and 1859, had as its aim the creation of a stable state prosperous enough to dominate Italy. In some respects, stability was achieved by methods that would not have been approved by the English statesmen he so much admired. Mazzinian democrats were persecuted, the Mazzinian press was suppressed, and parliament was overridden when it did not serve the purposes of the Prime Minister. For example, in 1857, when the elections returned an unexpected right-wing majority, Cavour seized upon a series of dubious technicalities to unseat a number of the successful candidates and so reduce the right wing. In January 1855, Cavour held all three of the main posts in the administration: Prime Minister, Foreign Minister and Finance Minister.

Other policies for creating stability were more liberal. A string of administrative reforms – in the financial departments (1852), in the foreign office (1853), and those of Alphonso La Marmora in the army – increased efficiency and removed those conservative elements hostile to Cavour. Further anti-clerical measures – notably the suppression of 152 **monasteries** and 1,700 **benefices** in 1855 – further restricted the influence of the Church, but also added the equivalent of an extra £145,640 to the state's income.

Cavour and economic modernisation

The most spectacular achievement of the decade consisted of the foundations that were laid for Piedmontese commercial and industrial prosperity. Already, as Minister of Finance and Commerce, Cavour had concluded a string of free-trade treaties. These were concluded with Belgium, with France and with Britain. They had the dual purpose of forging international links with the more advanced states of western Europe, and of attracting into Piedmont the raw materials and machinery necessary for its development. In the same capacity, Cavour floated large internal and

---

Urbano Rattazzi (1808–1873)
Piedmontese Minister of the Interior (1848). Minister of Justice (1853). Minister of the Interior (1859) but retired over the handing over of Nice and Savoy to France. Prime Minister (1862 and 1867).

Alphonso La Marmora (1804–1876)
Piedmontese general, active in the wars of 1848–49. Minister of War (1849). Commanded Piedmontese forces in the Crimea (1855) and in the campaigns of 1859 and 1861. Prime Minister (1864). Defeated at Custoza (1866).

Monasteries: Buildings in which a group of monks live together and carry out their religious practices.

Benefices: Posts and offices occupied by priests, together with the income derived from them.

foreign loans to pay off the war indemnity owed to the Austrians and to finance the industrial projects of the government. The level of government expenditure on such projects, as well as the long-term effects of the policy, may be judged from the fact that the public debt of Piedmont rose, between 1847 and 1859, from 120 million lire (Italian currency) to 725 million.

It would, of course, be misleading to refer to Piedmont in 1859 as a 'modern industrial power', but it had produced a number of impressive projects to advertise its status as the most advanced of the Italian states. Of Italy's 1,798 kilometres of railway track in 1859, Piedmont had 819 kilometres. Italy's first steamship, the 'Sicilia', was built in Genoa in 1855, and Italy's first home-produced railway locomotives were built in the same year. Further schemes were in progress for the construction of the Mont Cenis tunnel through the Alps, and for the modernisation of the port of Genoa. In the course of the 1850s, Piedmont's trade trebled in value. By the end of the 1850s, therefore, Piedmont had effectively claimed first place in Italy, not only in terms of constitutions and of military leadership, but in material terms as well.

---

1. What evidence is there for regarding Piedmont as a progressive and modern state in the period 1849–1855?

2. In what respects, if any, was Piedmont better qualified to lead Italy in the early 1850s than any of the other Italian states?

3.2 Why did Piedmont participate in the Crimean War and what did it achieve by its participation?

Piedmontese motives

Cavour's most important contribution to the liberation of Italy was that he was able to place the 'Italian question' firmly into the general context of European diplomacy. This was the forum in which the 1815 settlement had been shaped, and the only forum in which that settlement could be revised. It was not until the outbreak of the Crimean War in 1854, however, that a real opportunity presented itself. It was a bold step for a minor power such as Piedmont to intervene in a European conflict such as this, and it is not surprising that some historians have seen this as a masterstroke by Cavour, supported by Victor Emmanuel. The historians Massimo Salvadori and Derek Beales, however, have laid the stress differently. In their view, much of the initiative came from the British and the French, who felt that Austria would be more likely to send troops to the Crimea if it were assured that Piedmont would be committed there too, and thus unable to attack them in the rear. Denis Mack Smith moves even further from the traditional interpretation, viewing the plan for intervention primarily as the brainchild of Victor Emmanuel who, fretting at the constitutional restraints imposed upon him, saw war as a good opportunity to reassert his royal authority.

The Piedmontese contribution

Whatever the process by which the decision was reached, by the end of 1854 Piedmont had concluded an agreement with the allies by which 18,000 Piedmontese troops would fight in the Crimea. Subsequently, Piedmont would be entitled to a place at the congress at which peace would eventually be made. Neither the military intervention nor the Congress of Paris was as successful for the Italian cause as Italian historians have sometimes claimed.

Piedmont's military contribution to the war was limited. La Marmora's troops gave a good account of themselves at the battle of the Chornaya (August 1855) and, in their own eyes, did something to restore the prestige lost at Custoza and Novara. On the other hand, they scarcely played a key role, and the official line that 'about 2,000 of them were killed or died of disease' conceals the fact that not more than 30 of that number actually died of their wounds. Similarly, Cavour travelled to Paris for the peace conference, in 1856, still greatly inexperienced in the ways of 'great power' diplomacy, and with hopes that were never likely to be realised. His first aim was for territorial compensation for Piedmont's efforts, possibly in the shape of the Duchy of Parma. Such a measure was never seriously considered by the congress. His second aim was to obtain some commitment from the powers on the subject of the Austrian presence in Italy. He could not hope to obtain this from France which had troops of its own in Rome, and who could not contemplate renewed war so soon after the campaigns against Russia.

Neapolitan: The adjective used to describe something or someone coming from, or relating to, Naples.

It is true that the British representative, Lord Clarendon, attacked Austrian excesses and Papal and **Neapolitan** misgovernment in harsher terms than Cavour could have used. It was a measure of Cavour's inexperience, however, that he imagined that Clarendon might be speaking for his government. The British were soon to make it clear that they had no intention of intervening actively in so controversial a continental matter. In the context of 1856, Cavour had failed to achieve a diplomatic initiative and had not created the conditions necessary for a military solution to the problem of the Austrian presence.

1. What role did Piedmont play in the Crimean War?

2. How successful was Piedmontese participation in the Crimean War?

3.3 How was Piedmont able to launch a war against Austria in 1859?

Relations between Piedmont and Austria, 1856–1859

One result of the events in Paris in 1856 was a significant increase in Piedmontese confidence in her dealings with Austria. As a result of the peace conference, Cavour no doubt felt that the sympathy of Britain and France would, at the very least, be sufficient to deter Austria from any threatening ambitions. So it seemed, for Austrian policy in its provinces of Lombardy and Venetia, from 1856, was more conciliatory. The policy of confiscating the property of exiles was relaxed, and an amnesty for political prisoners was announced in 1857. Victor Emmanuel's famous speech of January 1859, in which he declared that he could not stop his ears to the 'cry of grief' (*grido di dolore*) that came from the neighbouring provinces, must have tested Austrian nerves to breaking point. It may have been instrumental in making them blunder into war later that year.

Piedmont and the nationalists

Another undoubted effect of the *grido di dolore* speech was to cement relations between the Piedmontese government and the nationalist exiles within Piedmont. Relations between Cavour and the exiled nationalists had been ambiguous since the Crimean War. The latter had formed the National Society in 1857, which boasted a membership of some 8,000 and whose main figures were Giuseppe La Farina, Giorgio Pallavicino and Daniele Manin, the hero of the former Venetian Republic. They were further convinced, by the intervention in the Crimean War, that Piedmont represented Italy's best hope, but they still entertained severe reservations about the sincerity of the state's leadership, and especially about that of Cavour. Manin had written in 1855, 'Convinced that above all Italy must be made, that this is the first and most important question, we say to the house of Savoy: "Make Italy and we are with you. If not, we are not."'

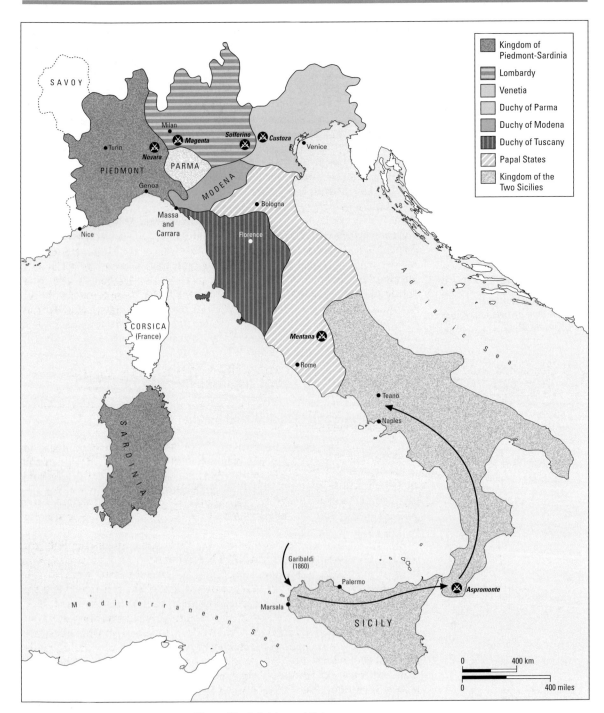

The political divisions of Italy

The Orsini affair and the Pact of Plombières

On the other hand, nothing was more likely to damage relations with France, certainly the most important factor in Cavour's calculations, than the assumption by Napoleon III that Piedmont was really serving the interests of a band of radicals. Although Cavour tried hard to consolidate the friendship formed in the Crimea, all was nearly ruined by Felice Orsini's terrorist attack in January 1858. The Orsini affair was a mysterious business, but there seems little doubt that Napoleon III's first reaction was one of great bitterness towards a Piedmontese government that had allowed Orsini to avoid arrest and to reach France.

At this stage, Victor Emmanuel performed one of his greatest services to Italy. In giving a brave reply to the attacks of the Emperor, he presented Piedmont as the best guarantee in Italy against the excesses of the radicals. These claims, combined with Napoleon's long-standing, if vague, desire to 'do something for Italy', calmed the Emperor. A visit by his confidant, Dr Conneau, to Turin (June 1858) raised hopes of direct co-operation between the two states against Austria. Thereafter progress was rapid, culminating in the secret meeting between Cavour and Napoleon III at Plombières in July. There plans were drawn up for French military intervention, resulting in the expulsion of Austria from Lombardy and Venetia, the enlargement of Piedmont and an Italy made up of four major power blocs. It seems highly likely that the terms of the Plombières agreement represented the views of Napoleon III, rather than those of Cavour. One is led, once more, to the view of Cavour as an **opportunist** willing to accept conditions of this sort to achieve what he had long known to be an essential precondition of the liberation of northern Italy, namely the military intervention of France.

Opportunist: A politician who does not act according to pre-established principles, but who adapts his policies to take advantage of specific opportunities as they arise.

3.4 How successful was the war of 1859 from the point of view of the Piedmontese government?

The Piedmontese war effort

For many years, the war of 1859 was traditionally viewed by Italian writers as a war of national liberation, cunningly contrived by dedicated Italians and finally betrayed at Villafranca by a cynical foreigner. Instead, study of the Piedmontese and Austrian war efforts should show how essential the part played by the French forces was to the achievement of even the limited success of 1859.

Italian reaction to the outbreak of war sheds some interesting light on the extent of Italian enthusiasm. The Piedmontese mobilisation was half-hearted. Not only was there a tendency to leave the hard work to the French, but also a distinct reluctance on the part of the conservative army officers to arm large numbers of men at a time when Piedmont was full of dangerous radical exiles. Where there was enthusiasm it was not always for the cause of nationalism. Victor Emmanuel felt himself, writes historian Mack Smith, 'a new man, powerful again, and free from interfering civilians'. Indeed, relations between King and Prime Minister were rarely worse than at this time when Victor Emmanuel directed affairs in Turin. For one reason or another, the numbers of the Piedmontese army fell 40% short of the figure agreed at Plombières, and they were not supplemented by a flood of patriotic volunteers from other parts of Italy. Victor Emmanuel had boasted of 200,000 such volunteers rallying to his cause, but only about 10% of that total materialised.

The Austrian war effort

Fortunately for Piedmont, the Austrian campaign was also faulty. The command of their forces was left by the Emperor to the 'courtier soldiers' Count von Grüünne and Count Gyulai, rather than to the more able Benedek or Hess. Their mobilisation was carried out at the slow pace of the

Napoleonic Wars, allowing the French ten days to move their troops into Piedmont by rail. The mobilisation could not be more than partial, given the need to leave large numbers of troops in other parts of the Empire, especially in Hungary, in anticipation of possible trouble there. The force of 90,000 that eventually assembled in Italy was considerably smaller than the Franco-Piedmontese force that faced it.

The main battles of the campaign that followed – at Magenta (4 June) and at Solferino (24 June) – were predominantly French engagements. Indeed, not a single Piedmontese soldier lost his life at Magenta, although on the day of Solferino the Piedmontese army was involved nearby in a subsidiary engagement at San Martino. It was, therefore, logical and perfectly in keeping with the previous history of the 'Italian question' that peace should be made when and how the intervening power dictated.

Villafranca and the resignation of Cavour

The armistice concluded at Villafranca on 11 July 1859 emphasises the extent to which the fate of Italy depended upon wider European consider-ations. Not only were the negotiations limited to the rulers of France and Austria, but Napoleon III was motivated more strongly by events in the Rhineland than by those in Italy. It seems likely, however, that he was also motivated, to some extent, by logical misgivings about Piedmont's conduct of the war. It seemed unlikely that the small kingdom would be able to fulfil its promise to pay France's campaign expenses if the war continued for much longer. Piedmont's commanders had virtually no plans nor much equipment for the prolonged siege warfare that would now be necessary if the line of Austrian fortresses on the borders of Venetia (the 'Quadrilateral') were to be attacked. Finally, it was becoming increasingly clear that Cavour had plans for the central Italian duchies that went far beyond the terms of the Plombières agreement.

The terms of the armistice transferred Lombardy, minus the important border fortresses of Peschiera and Mantua, to France on the assumption that it would transfer the territory in turn to Piedmont. The rulers of Tuscany and Modena, who had fled at the news of Magenta, were to be restored, and the principle of a **confederacy** under Papal leadership was reaffirmed. Venetia, of course, remained in Austrian hands. The attitude of Victor Emmanuel to the settlement was ambiguous; that of Cavour was not. Meeting his monarch for the first time in weeks, he railed against the terms of the armistice, called the king '"traitor" and worse', and, in desper-ation, advised that Piedmont should fight on alone. When the king wisely rejected such foolish advice, Cavour resigned his office.

The issue of the Central Duchies

Even as these events were taking place, it was becoming increasingly clear that the terms of Villafranca could never be implemented in full. The major difficulty would be the restoration of the rulers of central Italy. In his main piece of direct co-operation with the National Society, Cavour had connived at the establishment of provisional administrations in the central Italian territories, in the name of 'Italy and Victor Emmanuel'. By taking such action in an area designated at Plombières as strictly beyond Piedmontese control, Cavour was already violating the agreement and reinterpreting it in a fashion more favourable to his own state. The king seems to have had no prior knowledge of the operation and regarded it as madness to risk the alienation of his ally at such a vital stage in the campaign.

Cavour's resignation after Villafranca left his 'commissioners' in Tuscany, Parma and Modena in an awkward position. Faced with the alternatives of

Confederacy: A political alliance or association made up of more or less equal members.

Luigi Farini (1812–1866)
Moderate nationalist and associate of Cavour. Piedmontese Minister for Public Instruction (1851). Provisional Governor of Modena (1859), in which capacity he promoted the attachment of that territory to Piedmont. Minister of Commerce in Cavour's last cabinet (1861).

Bettino, Baron Ricasoli (1809–1880)
Prominent Tuscan landowner and agriculturalist. Active in the overthrow of the Grand Duke in 1859, and as 'dictator' of Tuscany was instrumental in its attachment to the Kingdom of Italy.

Annexation: The act of incorporating new territory into a state.

1. What factors enabled Piedmont to launch a war against Austria only ten years after the Piedmontese defeats of 1848 and 1849?

2. 'Cavour's foreign policy in the 1850s was over-ambitious and unrealistic, and it did not achieve its aims.' Is this judgement too harsh?

acting on their own initiatives, or abandoning their positions, they did the former. Luigi Farini had himself elected dictator in Parma, Modena and Romagna, which he declared united under their old Latin title of 'Emilia'. In Florence, the capital of Tuscany, a provisional government under Baron Ricasoli played the same role. It declared that it would never tolerate the return of the former rulers and that its intention was to become 'part of a strong Italian kingdom under the constitutional sceptre of King Victor Emmanuel'. Further reforms, in both Emilia and Tuscany, brought the currencies and customs duties of those territories into line with those of Piedmont.

The plebiscites of 1860

The actions of Farini and Ricasoli were, indeed, brave and valuable for the Italian cause, but they draw attention once again to the contribution made by Napoleon III with his military intervention. Not only were his armies indirectly responsible for the original flight of the rulers of Tuscany, Parma and Modena, but it was he, in the negotiations at Zurich to formalise the armistice of Villafranca, who insisted that no force should be used to implement the terms relating to central Italy. This ruled out the dangers of Austrian or French intervention on behalf of the former rulers, but made it hard for Piedmont to enforce its own union with the territories. The answer to this problem lay in combining this piece of unfinished business with another.

The section of the Plombières agreement whereby France would receive Nice and Savoy as repayment for its military aid, had been ignored at Villafranca as France's undertaking to clear the Austrians from Lombardy and Venetia, remained unfulfilled. Now it was resurrected in a Franco-Piedmontese agreement concluded in Turin in March 1860. It was decided that Savoy and Nice on the one hand, and Emilia and Tuscany on the other, should hold plebiscites to decide their future allegiances. In both cases, the result was emphatic. In Emilia, the voting was 426,000 to 1,506 in favour of **annexation** by Piedmont; in Tuscany, the margin was 366,571 to 14,925, although a total of 153,000 abstentions served as a reminder that Tuscans remained attached to their separate historical and cultural traditions.

The events of 1859–60 represented neither complete success nor complete disappointment for Piedmont. Its area and population were doubled as a result of war and diplomacy. Both of these methods of expansion, however, had depended, crucially, upon the aid of France, and Piedmont now faced the task of defending and consolidating her gains without the direct protection of its ally.

3.5 What were the political aims and methods of Giuseppe Garibaldi?

The rapid progress of the Italian cause from the apparent deadlock of early 1860 was largely the responsibility of one remarkable man. Giuseppe Garibaldi was born in Nice (4 July 1807) and was associated, from about 1834, with the romantic and conspiratorial nationalism of Mazzini's 'Young Italy'. His first efforts in the Italian cause – participation in an unsuccessful rising in Genoa – earned him a death sentence, passed in his absence. He fled to South America, where he established his reputation as a guerrilla fighter of genius. In 1848, his defence of Mazzini's Roman Republic earned him an international reputation. After further exile in America, and on his island home of Caprera off the coast of Sardinia, he fought for Piedmont in 1859 – or, as he saw it, for Italy against Austria.

Giuseppe Garibaldi depicted as the 'Liberator of Sicily' – painting by Auguste Etienne

His aims for Italy were simple. With a disregard for the constraints imposed either by international diplomacy or by economic backwardness, he worked for a free and unified state, preferably a republic, but a constitutional monarchy if necessary. His political views were confused, so confused that both the English Liberal, William Gladstone, and the Fascist dictator, Benito Mussolini, could claim him as a kindred spirit. The obituary of Garibaldi published in *The Times* (5 June 1882) passed an accurate judgement upon him.

'In politics, as in arms, his mind lacked the basis of a rudimentary education. He rushed to conclusions without troubling his head about arguments. His crude notions of democracy, of communism, of cosmopolitanism, or positivism, were jumbled together in his brain and jostled one another in hopeless confusion.'

Garibaldi's fame and achievement, however, rest upon his actions rather than his thought. His contribution to Italian unification falls halfway between those of the other two great Italian figures, Mazzini and Cavour. Mazzini kept the flame of Italian nationalism burning at the time of greatest adversity but, in material terms, achieved very little. Cavour achieved much, but had to dirty himself and his reputation in the murky waters of European politics to do it. By his dashing and naïve reliance on direct military action, Garibaldi seemed to many to have avoided both of these traps. His greatest admirer among historians, G.M. Trevelyan, wrote in *Garibaldi and the Making of Italy* (1911) that his work should be 'an encouragement to all high endeavour amongst us in a later age, who, with our eyes fixed on realism and the doctrine of evolution, are in danger of losing faith in ideals'.

Why was Garibaldi able to launch a successful campaign in southern Italy in the aftermath of the 1859 war?

No event in the eleven year period (1859–70), during which the modern Italian state was effectively created, has so caught the imagination as Garibaldi's invasion of Sicily and the subsequent overthrow of the Neapolitan state. Certainly, his tactical expertise and personal charisma were major factors in the success of the Sicilian adventure but the roots of this success were more complicated.

The Sicilian revolt
Garibaldi did not initiate events in Sicily. The rising that took place on 4 April in Palermo, the chief city of the island, owed nothing to him or to Cavour. It was the work of a group of Mazzinian republicans, led by Francesco Crispi and Rosalino Pilo. As republicans, they had refused to identify with the war of the Piedmontese monarchy in the previous year, and now Cavour returned the compliment by ignoring their approaches to him. The support that the rising received in Palermo was due to a combination of national and local factors. It was partly a result of the excitement generated by the events of 1859, but more important was the disappointment felt at the continued conservatism of the young King Francis II, newly succeeded to the throne of Naples.

The major difference between this outburst and its Mazzinian forerunners was that the Palermo revolt was quickly taken up in the countryside by the peasantry. Their motives derived entirely from local affairs, and their violent protests were directed as much against the landlords who raised their rents and charged them for the privilege of grinding their own corn, as against the Neapolitan troops who were sent to restore order.

Encouraged by these circumstances, Garibaldi began to prepare for the passage to Sicily. With just over 1,000 volunteers – mainly of middle-class

Francesco Crispi (1819–1901)
Sicilian radical, active in the events of 1848, and in the Sicilian revolt of 1859–60. Subsequently became a politician of national significance and served as Prime Minister of Italy (1887–90 and 1894).

and professional origin and very few of them from further south than Tuscany – he sailed from Genoa in two ancient steamers and landed at Marsala on 11 May. He was aided by the presence of a squadron of ships of the Royal Navy, actually concerned with the safety of local British property, but wrongly supposed by the patrolling Neapolitan navy to be allies of Garibaldi. The arrival of these forces proved to be too much for the harassed Neapolitan troops. On 15 May, Garibaldi had a substantial success at Calatafimi. Palermo fell to him on 30 May and, shortly afterwards, agreement was reached with the Neapolitan commanders for the withdrawal of their troops across the straits to the mainland.

The conquest of Naples

The gallant and romantic Sicilian adventure now took on a succession of more sinister international implications. If Garibaldi were to follow the fleeing troops on to the Neapolitan mainland, why should he not beat them again? If he did so, what was to prevent him from crossing the border from Naples into the Papal States? If he did that, what could prevent a major international crisis involving the French garrison in Rome and, possibly, other Catholic powers?

None of these prospects was very attractive to the government of Piedmont, whose attitude to the Sicilian expedition, as a whole, has been the subject of controversy. Naturally, the 'nationalist' interpretation has been that Cavour and his government gave Garibaldi all the help they reasonably could without raising a storm of international, diplomatic protest. In reality, Garibaldi received so little help from the government that some would-be volunteers had to be sent home for lack of funds to feed them, and the ships that transported the 'thousand' to Sicily had to be

A cartoon which appeared in an Italian political magazine in May 1860, under the title 'A forbidden fruit'. Eve (Cavour) and the serpent (Garibaldi) discuss which of them shall pluck the apple (Sicily).

Why should the artist portray 'Europa' as blindfolded and unaware of the dispute over Sicily?

Arsenal: Building where weapons and pieces of military equipment are stored.

stolen. The government even refused the release of 12,000 of Garibaldi's own guns stored in a police **arsenal** in Milan.

The role of Victor Emmanuel, in this confused period of the *Risorgimento*, is difficult to define with certainty, but it seems likely that his was the crucial contribution. He undoubtedly felt dissatisfied with the limits imposed upon his Italian authority and influence at Villafranca, and with France's disapproving attitude over the Central Duchies. The British ambassador in Turin probably captured the King's state of mind when he wrote that he 'has no head for anything but the sword and the horse, looks forward with glee to drawing the one and riding the other, no matter where'. There is clear evidence that Victor Emmanuel was in contact, during this period, with Garibaldi and even with Mazzini, and he seems also to have toyed with the idea of obtaining Venetia, either by war or by purchase. It is hard to resist the conclusion that he did all this, not through any preconceived principles of unification, but rather through a restless desire to continue the extension and enlargement of his political influence in Italy.

Why then, if it did not support Garibaldi, did the government allow the expedition to gather on Piedmontese soil and to sail from a Piedmontese port? The answer seems to be provided by Cavour in a letter to his ambassador in Paris the day after the expedition had landed in Sicily. 'I could not stop his going, for force would have been necessary. And the ministry is in no position to face the immense unpopularity which would have been drawn upon it had Garibaldi been prevented.' Cavour's ministry did, indeed, face a major cabinet revolt at that time, in protest against the handing over of Nice and Savoy to France. Thus, torn between his dislike for Garibaldi's radicalism and the dangers of international objections, and the alternative danger of offending the many Italians who loved and admired Garibaldi, Cavour kept his mouth shut and his options open and waited upon the outcome.

How did Piedmont respond to Garibaldi's success?

The astonishing success of the 'thousand' forced Cavour's hand. A successful invasion of Naples by the *Garibaldini* would at best lead to a prestigious, radical regime in the south, disputing the leadership of Italy with Piedmont. At worst, it might precipitate a further international war in Italy over the status of the Papacy. Cavour clearly outlined the dangers of the moment. 'If Garibaldi passes over to the mainland and seizes the Kingdom of Naples and its capital, as he has done with Sicily and Palermo, he becomes absolute master of the situation. King Victor Emmanuel loses more or less all his prestige; in the eyes of the great majority of Italians he is no more than Garibaldi's friend. With the resources of a kingdom of nine million inhabitants at his disposal, surrounded as he is by irresistible popular prestige, it is impossible for us to struggle against him.'

Garibaldini: Term used to describe the followers of Giuseppe Garibaldi.

Cavour's first attempts to avert such disaster went sadly wrong. Agents were sent into the Kingdom of the Two Sicilies to stir up a pro-Piedmontese revolt that would pre-empt Garibaldi, but they only encountered the general apathy that had bedevilled generations of Italian revolutionaries. On 22 August 1860, Garibaldi finally crossed the Straits of Messina and landed on mainland Neapolitan territory. With the general population showing no serious inclination to protect him against the invaders, Francis II abandoned Naples on 6 September, and the *Garibaldini* occupied the city the following day. Cavour rose to the occasion with probably the greatest piece of opportunism of his career. On 12 September, he informed the European powers that Piedmont had no option but to intervene in the Papal territories to restore order. Opposition from Papal forces was brushed aside six days later at Castelfidardo and, by 1 October, the Neapolitan forces between the two sets of invaders had ceased to resist.

Cartoon from *Punch*, 1860.
Giuseppe Garibaldi trying to
persuade Pope Pius IX that the
Cap of Liberty would be far more
comfortable than the Papal
crown.

**What issues does this cartoon
raise about obstacles to Italian
unification?**

A GOOD OFFER.

GARIBALDI. "TAKE TO THIS CAP, PAPA PIUS. YOU WILL FIND IT MORE COMFORTABLE THAN
YOUR OWN."

**1. What were the results of
Garibaldi's expedition to
southern Italy in 1860?**

**2. Why did Garibaldi's tactic of
direct military action achieve so
much in 1860 and so little at any
other time?**

**3. 'By the end of 1860,
Garibaldi had done more than
Cavour to bring about a united
Italy.' Do you agree with this
statement?**

At a dramatic meeting at Teano, north of the city of Naples (26 October),
Garibaldi faced the choice of acknowledging the supremacy of the King of
Piedmont, or fighting him. He chose to hand over his conquests to Victor
Emmanuel and to retire, voluntarily, to his island home of Caprera.
Plebiscites were held with the now customary haste. By the end of 1860
these had sanctioned the union, not only of the Kingdom of the Two Sicilies,
but also of the Papal territories of Umbria and the Marches, with Piedmont-
Sardinia, now dignified by the new title of the Kingdom of Italy.

3.6 To what extent should Cavour be regarded as a champion of Italian unification?
A CASE STUDY IN HISTORICAL INTERPRETATION

The events of 1850–70 created the modern state of Italy, and thus remain
of great symbolic and emotional importance to it. For that reason, the
history of the *Risorgimento* has often been 'borrowed' and reinterpreted by
subsequent generations. Various schools of Italian historians, with very
different political and intellectual agendas, have found reasons to assume

that the most prominent Italian leaders of the period shared a common vision. Coming to the fore in the early days of Italian statehood, and equally acceptable under Benito Mussolini's Fascist regime, nationalist historians were concerned to establish the credentials of the new state, and to represent its creation as a coherent movement of like-minded patriots. Writers who regarded Italian unification as 'the most important fact of the 19th century' (such as D. Zanichelli) naturally regarded Cavour as a kindred spirit and as a dedicated nationalist politician.

A second sympathetic school consisted of those 'liberal' historians who saw the *Risorgimento* as an important element in the defeat of autocracy and reaction, and in the triumph of **modernism**. Such a view was promoted by the Italian historian Benedetto Croce, in *A History of Italy, 1871–1915* (1929). For Croce, the methods and tactics of Cavour and other Italian leaders were fully justified by the end-product of the *Risorgimento*: a successful, modern, and essentially liberal Italian state. This view of the *Risorgimento* was understandably popular among English-speaking historians. While the British historian, G.M. Trevelyan (*Garibaldi's Defence of the Roman Republic*, 1907; *Garibaldi and the Thousand*, 1909; *Garibaldi and the Making of Italy*, 1911) portrayed Giuseppe Garibaldi as a great European liberal, as well as the enemy of tyranny and of unrepresentative government, others performed a similar service for Cavour. A.J. Whyte (*The Political Life and Letters of Cavour*, 1930) and the American W.R. Thayer (*The Life and Times of Cavour*, 1911) emphasised the dedication of the great Piedmontese statesman to the national cause. Throughout, the dominant impression is that the statesman, the radical and the guerrilla leader may have differed in tactics and in their immediate priorities, but that each provided an essential element to the common goal of Italian unification.

The claim that Cavour should be set apart from Italian nationalist leaders has come largely from the English historian, Denis Mack Smith. Mack Smith caused controversy among Italian historians by challenging the traditional reputations of many of the Italians prominent in the movement for unification, and in particular by distancing Cavour from the nationalist cause. In *Cavour and Garibaldi, 1860* (1954) and in *Cavour* (1985), the Piedmontese statesman emerges as a cunning politician, without any ideological attachment to the principle of unification and primarily concerned with the **aggrandisement** of Piedmont-Sardinia. Similarly, Mack Smith shows little sympathy towards the view of Victor Emmanuel as an idealistic patriot and father of his country (*Victor Emmanuel, Cavour and the Risorgimento*, 1971).

In geographical terms, the origins of Garibaldi, Mazzini and Cavour were very similar. All three were born in territory which, after 1815, belonged to the kingdom of Piedmont, and each was born within five years of the others (Mazzini 1805, Garibaldi 1807, Cavour 1810). In social and economic terms, however, all the advantages lay with Cavour. Born into a family of the Piedmontese nobility, his background was as much French as it was Italian, and was open to the broader influences of western European thought. The young Cavour derived his ideas largely from the great economic theorists of the day, such as Adam Smith and David Ricardo. His extensive foreign travels – in France, Britain and Switzerland – also shaped his political and economic views. Observation of Britain's industrial growth helped to turn him into a broad-minded conservative with views similar to those of his greatest political 'hero', Sir Robert Peel. Back home, he implemented these views in economic enterprises, such as the formation of the Lake Maggiore Steamboat Company and the foundation, with others, of the Bank of Genoa and the Bank of Turin. He also spread these ideas through journalism, founding *Il Risorgimento* (1847), a liberal journal popular in Piedmont and with the Italian refugees who flocked into Piedmont from other parts of the

Modernism: New ideas and methods, especially when they are contrasted with earlier thinking.

Aggrandisement: The act of making oneself or one's country larger and/or more important.

peninsula. He came to politics relatively late, was elected to Piedmont's first constitutional assembly (June 1848), and his rapid rise owed more to his progressive economic views than to any vision of Italian nationhood.

Some historians still view Cavour as deliberately working towards the modernisation, liberation and unification of Italy. It is extremely important, therefore, to understand the nature of his 'liberalism' and his 'nationalism' correctly. Of the former, Massimo Salvadori has written, in *Cavour and the Unification of Italy* (1961), that 'Cavour believed in liberty, in responsibility, and in the ability of the educated individual to act responsibly on the basis of his own decisions.' Yet this man achieved his aims partly by bribing newspapers and rigging elections. Every major step of his diplomatic career was taken without consultation with parliament. It is perhaps easier to consider what Cavour did not believe in. As early as 1835 he had written that 'I am persuaded that the *juste milieu* is the only policy right in the circumstances, capable of saving society from the two rocks which threaten to break it – anarchy and despotism'. His 'liberal' policies, therefore, were a means of avoiding the main dangers that he felt threatened Piedmont, and perhaps Italy. These were the tyranny of the traditionalist, autocratic state and the dogmatism of a reactionary Church and, on the other hand, the dangerous extremism of Mazzini and the other left-wing radicals active in Italian politics.

The question of Cavour's nationalism has produced even greater controversy. Historians have claimed, on the one hand, that the unification of Italy was his aim from the beginning of his career and, on the other, that he was mainly interested in the expansion and consolidation of his own Piedmontese state. Denis Mack Smith has maintained that, as late as 1858, 'he [Cavour] still could not accept Mazzini's idea of a united Italy. So long as he obtained Lombardy and Venice he would dominate the peninsula, and that was enough.'

To understand Cavour's attitude to the question of Italian national unity, it may be best to view him as a man who lacked the power to dominate events, or to direct them consistently towards any preconceived goal. Rather, Cavour was a practical politician with aims, originally limited, but modified and expanded by developments over which he had little control. We find a clue, perhaps, in the letter written by Manin to Giorgio Pallavicino (September 1856). 'We must work incessantly to form public opinion, because as soon as opinion is clear and forceful, Cavour I am sure will follow it. I think Cavour to be too intelligent and too ambitious to refuse the Italian enterprise if public opinion demands it strongly enough.' It does appear to be the case that Cavour's views underwent a significant change in the last stages of his life, driven by the pressure of the events taking place around him. In 1860, with his bid for control of northern Italy checked at Villafranca, Cavour lost the initiative in Italian politics to Garibaldi. Forced to annex the southern provinces to keep them out of radical hands, he found himself having to adopt Garibaldi's nationalist programme. He seems then to have realised that the impetus towards unity – away from the greater Piedmont that had been his original goal – was unstoppable. In one of his last parliamentary speeches Cavour surprised his audience with the assertion that, in the long term, it was desirable and inevitable that Rome should become the capital of Italy.

In a sense, therefore, Cavour eventually adopted the geographical programme of Mazzini and of Garibaldi. He never accepted their political programme, however, and firmly imposed his own political vision upon the Italian peninsula as a whole. The communist writer, Antonio Gramsci, fully appreciated this fact when he wrote, in *Il Risorgimento* in 1949, that Cavour 'conceived unity as an increasing of the Piedmontese state and of the patrimony of the dynasty, not at base a national movement, but a royal conquest'.

1. What different views have historians taken of the role that Cavour played in the unification of Italy?

2. What alternatives have historians put forward to the view of Cavour as a champion of Italian unification?

3.7 What problems faced the new Italian state in the 1860s?

The death of Cavour and its aftermath

The new kingdom of Italy, officially in existence from March 1861, had to face the future without the talents of the man who had done more than anyone to establish it. Cavour died unexpectedly on 6 June 1861, exhausted by the problems and tensions of the previous few years. His aims had undoubtedly been different from those of Mazzini and Garibaldi, and his relations with his King had been cool and suspicious. By his masterly flexibility, however, in the face of great political and emotional forces that he could not control directly, he deserved the place with which he was credited by the English poet, George Meredith (1828–1909), in the creation of Italy:

'We think of those
Who blew the breath of life into her frame:
Cavour, Mazzini, Garibaldi: Three:
Her Brain, her Soul, her Sword; and set her free

From ruinous discords.'

Unfortunately, Italy was far from being 'free from ruinous discords'. It had been formed hastily, imperfectly and against the will of many, and now had to face the cost of Cavour's policies. In Cavour's place followed a succession of men: Baron Ricasoli (1861–62), Urbano Rattazzi (March–December 1862), Luigi Farini (1862–63), Marco Minghetti (1863–64) and Alphonso La Marmora (1864–66). None of these was of the calibre of their predecessor, and most of them had been kept relatively ignorant of the details of government by Cavour's virtual monopoly of the major cabinet posts.

The cost of unity

Of the three main problems that faced these men, the most glaring was the state of the Italian economy. The new kingdom had to cope with a huge deficit of 2,450 million lire, incurred by Cavour to carry through his policies of 1856 (which cost 50 million lire) and 1859 (which cost a further 250 million). It also inherited the debts of the smaller regimes that it had helped to oust from other parts of Italy. It was further assumed that a modern state would need certain trappings, such as new roads, railways and military equipment. The construction of a sizeable modern navy, in particular, was a luxury when Italy's most likely enemy, Austria, was predominantly a land power. The result was heavy and unpopular taxation, such as a flour tax proposed in 1865, and the negotiation of large foreign loans often on humiliating terms. By the middle of the 1860s, more than a third of Italian government bonds were in foreign hands and most Italian railway shares were owned by non-Italians.

Agrarian and industrial backwardness

Italy faced these problems with its main economic activity, agriculture, so deeply in debt that an estimated 30% of each year's product was eaten up by repayments. Agricultural methods were so outdated that the economist Nassau Senior considered that cereal production in the south had scarcely increased its output since the days of the Roman Empire. Furthermore, it proved impossible to extend Cavour's principles of financial and industrial modernisation to the rest of Italy. Conservative attitudes in central and southern Italy included a distrust of paper money and a condemnation of financial borrowing and lending as immoral.

Agriculture so dominated the lives of the working classes that the census of 1861 showed only three million people employed in industrial production, of whom 80% were women or children sharing their time between this and agriculture. The textile industry and the production of some chemicals, such as sulphur, had potential but, in an age dominated by coal, Italy lacked sources of energy until the development of hydro-electric power enabled it to exploit its considerable water resources.

The nature of the 'southern question'

Italy's economic difficulties were rivalled by the 'southern question': the difficulties that arose from the social, economic and political diversity of the Italian regions. The huge majorities recorded in favour of unity, in 1860–61, conveyed a misleading impression. They constituted a vote against a number of things, like the tyranny and incompetence of the previous rulers and the lawlessness of rebellious peasants. They probably also represented a considerable degree of electoral malpractice. An observer of the Nice plebiscite, for instance, noted that the slips necessary for a 'no' vote were often in short supply and were sometimes missing altogether, and this was probably true in many cases in the south. What those who voted 'yes' were actually voting for was not absolutely clear.

United Italy could have taken one of at least two forms:

- a federal state, in which the regions retained much of their local autonomy,

- or a centralised one, wholly governed from one national capital.

Cavour seems to have considered both options but, in the last months of his life, he had firmly set his face against the federal solution. The reasons are not altogether clear. It is true that, at that time, federalism seemed to have failed in the world's greatest federal state, the USA, which stood on the verge of civil war in 1861. It is difficult to avoid the conclusion, however, that federalism was seen to threaten the dominant position of Piedmont within Italy, and that Cavour's decision was taken in order to impose a rapid solution upon a problem that he had not expected to arise so suddenly.

'Piedmontisation'

Italy thus became 'piedmontised' at an almost indecent rate. The legal system of Naples, for example, was revolutionised by the passage of 53 decrees in only two days, in February 1861. 'Piedmontisation' involved the division of the new kingdom into 53 provinces on the model of the French *départements*, each governed by a prefect. Customs, coinage, weights and measures were all standardised, in theory, although the illegal use of old coinage and measures persisted at least until the end of the century. The Italian constitution was, in effect, an expanded version of the Piedmontese constitution. The new assembly comprised 443 members, elected by a mere 150,000 voters, who fulfilled the dual qualification of paying 40 lire per year in taxes, and of being literate. Thus, on average, each deputy was elected by about 300 voters.

'Piedmontisation' had two great drawbacks. One was the daunting degree of ignorance that existed in all parts of Italy about the other parts. In particular, the ignorance of the north about conditions in Naples and Sicily extended to all levels of government. Cavour himself, although he had visited France, Britain and Switzerland, never travelled further south than Tuscany. The policy resulted, therefore, in a bizarre series of misconceptions and mistakes. Compulsory education was prescribed for southern

Convents: The buildings where nuns lived and carried out their religious existence.

Mafia: A secret society originating in Sicily, and active there in opposition to Neapolitan rule.

Brigandage: The practice of bandits (brigands) who live by pillage and robbery.

---

1. What difficulties did the Italian government face in southern Italy as a result of the events of 1860?

2. Is it more accurate to regard the events of 1859–63 as 'Piedmontese expansion' or as 'Italian unification'?

3. To what extent, and in what respects, was the unification of Italy still incomplete at the time of Cavour's death in 1861?

Italy, where 90% of the population was illiterate, but it could not be paid for without attacking the property of the Church. The dissolution of 2,382 monasteries and **convents**, by 1866, provided some funds, but outraged local religious feelings and deprived the localities of charitable institutions run by the monks and nuns long before the state could afford to replace them. The jury system was introduced throughout the south despite the protests of local authorities that **Mafia** activity would make the corruption and intimidation of juries a simple matter.

The second drawback was a simple lack of resources, both financial and human. The south, it was fondly imagined by men who had never been there, was rich in minerals. Instead, it had proved a drain on the resources of the north. Piedmont, unlike Prussia in the case of German unification, had neither the income nor the trained manpower to administer its new territories effectively.

'The imposition of the Piedmontese administrative system,' concludes Denis Mack Smith, 'reinforced the impression that one region had virtually conquered the rest.' Predictably, the southern regions reacted as they had done against earlier injustices. What the national government referred to as 'campaigns for the suppression of **brigandage**' amounted to a full-scale civil war in the south. The issue was not effectively settled in the central government's favour until 1865, and the struggle claimed more Italian lives than all the battles of the *Risorgimento* put together. In 1863 alone the government committed 90,000 troops to peacekeeping operations in the south, far more than had ever taken the field against the Austrians.

It was not realistic to expect that such deep-rooted difficulties would be solved within a decade. The processes of road building, agricultural reform and educational improvement were still far from complete by the outbreak of the First World War. It is not surprising, therefore, that the official utterances of the Italian government sought to concentrate public attention on the third of the new kingdom's outstanding problems as little as possible.

3.8 By what means, and with what success, did the Italian state extend its influence over other Italian territories?

The Venetian question

The government of Victor Emmanuel owed much of its continued prestige, in 1861, to its opportunistic intervention in Naples, which had enabled it to be identified with the national cause. It was thus very difficult for the government, especially at a time of such extreme domestic difficulties, to ignore the fact that, in the eyes of the nationalists, there were still two very important pieces missing from the Italian 'jigsaw'. Upon taking office, Baron Ricasoli was quick to reassure Italians that 'we claim Rome as our natural capital and Venetia as an integral part of our national soil'. Rome and Venice, however, were not Naples. To gain either of them would mean dealing with one or more of the great powers at a time when nearly half of the Italian army was fighting its reluctant compatriots in the south.

The first moves towards a solution to the 'Venetian question' were therefore made by men to whom such diplomatic niceties were of little concern. Garibaldi and his 'party of action' assumed that what had worked in Naples, would work in Venetia. They were active in 1862, attempting to engineer an armed rising, and again in 1864, pinning their hopes this time on risings elsewhere in the Habsburg Empire which would draw Austrian troops out of Italy. In both cases, news leaked out. The protests of foreign diplomats caused the Italian government to intervene to thwart Garibaldi's plans.

The Prussian alliance and the war of 1866

Instead, like all the other component parts of the 'Italian question', except Naples, the Venetian question had to wait for a solution until the general mood of European politics was ready. The decline of Austria's relations with Prussia, in the course of the Schleswig-Holstein affair in 1864, alerted both Prussians and Italians to the common ground in their foreign policies, and to the common benefits that might result from action against Austria. Italian enthusiasm was not total. Victor Emmanuel continued to believe, in Mack Smith's words, that 'the important thing was to have a war, and as soon as possible', adding to his anti-constitutional motives of 1859 the desire to distract attention from the problems in the south. La Marmora, however, recalled the pitfalls involved in playing the role of junior partner to a major power, hence his offer to purchase Venetia from an anxious Austrian government for 1,000 million lire. The military faction in Vienna overrode the initial enthusiasm of the Austrian Emperor. The Italian government was left with little option but to enter into closer negotiations with Prussia.

By April 1866, General Govone's mission to Berlin had concluded a military agreement by which both sides undertook not to conclude a separate peace, thus hoping to avoid another Villafranca, and by which Italy was to receive Venetia as the reward for its role. On 20 June, four days after Prussia, Italy formally declared itself at war with Austria once more.

After the great gains of 1859–60, Italian expectations were high and the king himself was, according to one of his ministers, 'quite drunk with overconfidence'. In theory, the confidence was justified. Italy could expect to put some 250,000 men into the field against the 130,000 that the divided Austrian army could spare from its southern front. The fleet too, after the recent 'spending spree', could count 12 ironclad battleships of the most modern design, to Austria's seven. In reality, these advantages were to be outweighed by other factors. The Italian general staff was not notable for military skill and experience. Many, like the fleet's commander, Admiral Persano, owed their positions primarily to influence and corruption at Court. It was conveniently overlooked that it was not these men, but guerrillas and Frenchmen who had won the great battles of the *Risorgimento*. Even below the highest levels of command, organisation was so bad and planning so rudimentary that only about 25% of the army ever reached the front. Once there, the unfortunate troops found strategy paralysed by bitter personal rivalries between prominent officers, and by the presence of a monarch who insisted upon taking overall personal command, despite the opinion of General Cialdini that 'the King is wholly ignorant and incompetent'.

The initial confidence did not last long. On 24 June, La Marmora's and Cialdini's forces fought an indecisive action against a strong Austrian defensive position at Custoza, close to the 1848 battlefield. They then disintegrated, due to panic and to confused orders. The engagement wrecked the reputations of La Marmora and Cialdini and burst the 'bubble' of Italian military pride. A month later, Persano's fleet engaged the Austrian fleet off the island of Lissa in the Adriatic and, in the midst of similar confusion, lost three major ships including the 'Re d'Italia', the pride of the Italian navy. It was claimed, at Persano's **court martial**, that the fleet had fired 1,450 shells without scoring a major hit on the enemy.

Despite such failures, the crushing defeat inflicted by the Prussians

Court martial: The trial in a military court of a member of the armed forces who is charged with breaking a military law.

upon the Austrians at Sadowa (3 July) brought about an armistice (23 July) by which Italy gained Venetia after all. At the time, however, it was impossible to see the war as anything other than a miserable failure. Almost all the other aims of the government had been frustrated. It had achieved none of the heroism or glory necessary to weld the disparate parts of the country into a nationally conscious whole. The war had done great harm to the prestige of both the army and the monarchy, and Venetia had come into Italian hands, just as Lombardy had done in 1859, through the triumph of a foreign army. There had been no Venetian uprising in support of the Italian forces. Even the blindest of patriots could hardly fail to notice that the huge majority, recorded in the subsequent plebiscite in favour of union with the rest of Italy, hardly squared with the apathy that Venetians had shown during the war itself.

The problem of Rome: the failure of Garibaldi

The failures of 1866 rendered even bleaker the Italian government's prospects of establishing its capital in Rome. In the five years since Garibaldi had been checked on the Pope's frontiers, two main methods had been pursued for gaining access to Rome, but with little success.

The first solution had been that of the 'party of action'. Dismissing the power of the Papacy, Garibaldi seems to have regarded Rome as an easier target than Naples. He was wrong on three counts. Firstly, he would be forced to confront the French garrison as well as the small Papal army. Secondly, he would have to face the army of his own government, who could not permit 'banditry' to prejudice their diplomatic relations with France, and could not contemplate the humiliation of acquiring their capital city from the hands of a revolutionary. Thirdly, he was once more badly mistaken in hoping that his actions might spark off a popular revolt within the Papal territories. The Church was at the heart of the region's economy, and was unlikely to be attacked by the populace that it supported. Historian A.J. Whyte concluded, in *The Political Life and Letters of Cavour* (1930), 'The Church amused them, employed them and fed them, and to her they looked alike for consolation in trouble and material help in times of stress.'

Nevertheless, the idealism of Garibaldi and the highly ambiguous attitude of the King and some of his ministers, twice tempted the 'party of action' into projects that caused the government acute embarrassment. In August 1862, an expedition that could have been intercepted easily had the Italian fleet had clearer orders, landed at Aspromonte in Calabria. It had to be checked by government troops. Five years later, in October 1867, the provisional withdrawal of the French troops gave Garibaldi another opportunity. At Mentana (3 November), however, his forces were defeated by Papal troops, reinforced at the last moment by the hastily returning Frenchmen.

The problem of Rome: the search for a diplomatic solution

The second possible solution to the Roman question was by means of diplomacy. It seemed unlikely, however, that the Italian government, after a decade of anti-clericalism, would achieve much by direct negotiation with the Church. Throughout the *Risorgimento*, the reaction of the Papacy to changing social and political circumstances was, in the words of A.J. Whyte, 'to bind her medieval robe more closely about her'. This process of restating an inflexible position culminated in the publication, in December 1864, of the **encyclical** *Quanta Cura,* which listed a 'syllabus of errors' of 80 points. Among the 'errors' were the principles of liberty of conscience, state education, liberalism, constitutional government, and opposition to

Encyclical: A letter or order issued by the Pope to the bishops of the Church.

the temporal power of the Pope. It was an attack upon most of the progressive ideas of western Europe in the 19th century and, as such, was an embarrassment to all progressive Catholics. It was also a manifesto of opposition to most of the professed ideas of the Italian government.

Negotiations with France were rather more fruitful. Napoleon III had long regretted the expense and political inconvenience involved in protecting a stubborn and reactionary Pope, but could not agree to abandon him to the 'bandits' who had set up the Roman republic of 1849. After 1862, and the encounter at Aspromonte, it was possible to claim that the responsible Italian government effectively had Garibaldi under its control.

By 1864, therefore, the French were willing to enter into highly secret negotiations, which resulted in the so-called 'Convention of September'. France consented to remove its garrison from Rome, in return for an Italian undertaking to protect Papal territory from all external attack. A number of sympathetic commentators have been tempted to admire a move by which, in A.J. Whyte's words, 'the wolves were set to guard the fold'. Denis Mack Smith opposes that view, too, by pointing out that the Italian diplomats must either have been lying deliberately to the French, or else deliberately breaking their promises to the Italian electors concerning the acquisition of Rome.

The acquisition of Rome and subsequent relations with the Papacy

Whatever the motives behind it, the Convention of September did not bring the Italians any closer to making their capital in Rome. The withdrawal of French troops, in December 1866, was reversed by the Mentana fiasco less than a year later, and the situation remained one of stalemate and confrontation until 1870. Then, as usual, Italy's problems were resolved by European factors beyond Italy's control.

The drift of France towards war with Prussia offered two openings to Italy. The first was diplomatic when, in May 1870, Napoleon III sought a basis for an anti-Prussian alliance. For all its doubts about fighting against its most recent ally, Italy still suggested Rome as the price of its co-operation. For the French Catholics, that price remained too high. The outbreak of war, however, presented Italy with an opportunity that public opinion would not allow it to miss. France's Roman garrison could no longer be spared and by 19 August the evacuation was complete. The Prime Minister, Giovanni Lanza, still acted with great caution, waiting until the defeat of France at Sedan. The formal agreement of Spain, Austria and the Catholic German states, and the arrest of Mazzini, ensured that there would be no unfortunate side-effects. The modest Papal army was overcome in a brief engagement on 19 September 1870, as a result of which Rome was at last occupied by the Italian army.

The usual plebiscite (2 October) produced the usual result, a huge majority in favour of union with the rest of Italy (133,681 to 1,507). Once again, the result contradicted the previous indifference of the population, and a French officer in the Papal army, the Comte de Beaufort, published a detailed account of alleged dishonesty at the polls. This included the absence of 'no' voting slips, intimidation, plural voting and the introduction of non-qualified voters. His account is, perhaps, a fair representation of the plebiscites of the *Risorgimento*.

It was one thing to win Rome, and quite another to win the Church's acceptance of the fact. For instance, although stripped of his temporal powers, Pope Pius IX made his supreme act of defiance, in July 1870, by declaring the **doctrine of Papal Infallibility**. In May 1871, by the Law of Guarantees, the Italian government made a further gesture of conciliation

Doctrine of Papal Infallibility: The teaching that, as the Pope is God's representative on Earth, his decisions and utterances on doctrine express the will of God and cannot be questioned.

1. How did Venetia and Rome become parts of the united Italian state?

2. To what extent do the events of 1861–1870 support the view that Italian unification owed more to diplomacy than to nationalist fervour and Italian military skill?

as it sought to define the position of the Pope within the kingdom of Italy. The full spiritual jurisdiction of the Pope was recognised, freedom of communication with the Church throughout the world was confirmed, along with the liberty of appointment to all ecclesiastical offices, and the liberty of teaching. The Pope received an annual grant equivalent to £129,000, remained free of Italian taxation, and retained the full use of the Vatican and of Castel Gandolfo. Typically, Pius IX chose to remain 'a prisoner in the Vatican', and not until 1929 was the Italian state formally recognised by the Papacy.

Source-based questions: Cavour and Garibaldi's expedition in 1860

SOURCE A

You will see from Fanti's note that the government is very nearly in real trouble. Fanti was not wrong, as Minister of War, to wish to safeguard the pressing needs of defence. It is evident that the treaty could be the subject of very grave censures (on 10 May). In rushing through the cession [handing over] of Nice and Savoy without the least regard for the just sensibilities of the country, the French government has succeeded in destroying the influence of the government internally as well as externally: by indefinitely prolonging the negotiations over the frontiers, it will make the existence of the government impossible, and will only give more impetus and prestige to the opposition of Rattazzi and Garibaldi. [The French government] must realise that the position in which they have put me is not sustainable. I must have at least some argument to demonstrate that we have not forgotten to safeguard the interests of the country in these unhappy negotiations. Although one might say that Italy is grateful for the power that France has given us, yet a great number of deputies are not at all inclined to forget that the Peace of Villafranca left not only Venice but also Peschiera and Mantua to Austria, and that the annexation of central Italy was made not by France but against her.

If Fanti resigns, the existing government will not last more than a single day. Fanti is the only one among the existing ministers congenial to the King – and I have reason to believe that HM, who always has a weakness for Garibaldi and Rattazzi, is secretly looking to remove me from the direction of affairs. I would be well content to retire to Leri; but I am not the man to leave the country in the middle of the immense dangers which would spring from the rejection of the treaty. I am therefore disposed to carry the burden of power for a little longer – and the unpopularity.

I only ask that the Emperor gives me a little help to accomplish the thankless task I have undertaken, or at least not to make it more difficult for me.

Cavour to Nigra, Piedmontese ambassador in Paris, 24 April 1860

SOURCE B

Wednesday 2 May: Scovazzo informed me that Massimo D'Azeglio, Nigra and Hudson, the English Ambassador, were the people who are working with all their strength to keep Cavour Prime Minister. It now seems that serious opposition is being organised in the Senate over the two provinces of Nice and Savoy. The rebellion is spreading in Sicily.

Thursday 3 May: The news from Sicily is still favourable to the insurrection. Nicolari writes to me from Genoa that Garibaldi is going to leave in two days time with an elect band of young men. The Government is behaving rather passively, the clearest sign that the revolution has taken it by surprise. Public opinion in Turin is moving against Count Cavour: he may fall and never regain power.

From the political diary of the Piedmontese Senator, Asproni, May 1860

SOURCE C

Garibaldi has landed in Sicily. It is a great piece of luck that he did not pursue his idea of attacking the Pope. We cannot stop him making war against the King of Naples. Whether it turns out for the best or the worst, it was inevitable. He would have become dangerous in internal politics if he had been held back by force. What will happen now? It is impossible to predict. Will England help him? It is possible. Will France stop him? I believe not. And us? We cannot openly support him, neither can we restrain private efforts on his behalf. Therefore we have decided not to allow any new expeditions to be prepared from the ports of Genoa and Livorno, but not to stop the sending of arms and munitions, provided that it is carried out with a degree of prudence. I am not disguising all the inconvenience of this ill-defined line we are following, but I cannot think of an alternative which doesn't present more serious and dangerous prospects.

Cavour to Ricasoli, Royal Governor of Tuscany, 16 May 1860 (sent before Cavour received Source D).

SOURCE D

Just as the royal government ought to stop any attack on the Papal States at the moment, so it should tolerate and even give aid to the Sicilian insurrection, if that can be done covertly, and at least without compromising ourselves too much. We cannot sufficiently proclaim towards Europe the duty that binds Italians to help their compatriots who are subject to evil governments.

Ricasoli to Cavour, 15 May 1860

SOURCE E

I entirely agree with you about Garibaldi's expedition. I have nothing to add except that we must save appearances so as not to increase our diplomatic difficulties. France has shown less displeasure than I expected.

Cavour to Ricasoli, 23 May 1860

1. Explain briefly the following highlighted references that appear in the sources.

(a) 'In rushing through the cession of Nice and Savoy without the least regard for the just sensibilities of the country' (Source A)

(b) 'the Peace of Villafranca' (Source A)

(c) 'It is a great piece of luck that he did not pursue his idea of attacking the Pope' (Source C).

2. Study Sources B and C.

Does Source B provide convincing support for Cavour's profession of weakness (Source A)?

3. Compare the trustworthiness of Cavour's remarks in Sources A and C.

4. On the strength of these sources, and any other evidence known to you, discuss the assertion that 'until long after Garibaldi had sailed for Sicily, Cavour had no policy at all towards the expedition'.

Further Reading

Texts designed for AS and A2 Level students

Unification of Italy by John Gooch (Routledge, Lancaster Pamphlets, 1990)
The Unification of Italy 1815–70 by Andrina Stiles (Hodder & Stoughton, Access to History series, 1989)

More advanced reading

A History of Italy 1700–1860: the Social Constraints of Political Change by Stuart Woolf (Routledge, 1986)
Italy in the Age of the Risorgimento by Harry Hearder (Longman, History of Italy series, 1984)
The Risorgimento and the Unification of Italy by Derek Beales (Allen & Unwin, 1972)
Cavour by Denis Mack Smith (Methuen, 1985)
Mazzini by Denis Mack Smith (Yale University Press, 1994)
Cavour by Harry Hearder (Longman, Profiles in Power series, 1994)
The Italian Risorgimento: State, Society and National Unification by Lucy Riall (Routledge, Connections in History series, 1994) offers a good brief survey of recent trends in historical writing on this subject.

4 The failure of the liberal state and the rise of Italian Fascism, 1870–1922

Key Issues

- How stable and powerful was the Italian state in the 40 years before 1914?

- What impact did the First World War have on Italy?

- Why was Mussolini able to win power by October 1922?

4.1 How strong was parliamentary government in Italy between 1871 and 1914?

4.2 To what extent was the Italian economy modernised and strengthened between unification and the outbreak of the First World War?

4.3 By what means and with what success did Italy seek great power status in the years 1870–1914?

4.4 What factors contributed to the rise of Italian Fascism in the years after the First World War?

4.5 Historical Interpretation: How did Mussolini become dictator of Italy?

Framework of Events

1870	Incorporation of Rome into the Kingdom of Italy
1878	Death of Victor Emmanuel II; succession of Umberto I
1881	Treaty of Bardo establishes French protectorate over Tunisia and excludes Italian interests
1882	Triple Alliance between Italy, Germany and Austria
1887	Renewal of Triple Alliance. Introduction of protective tariffs. Massacre of Italian troops at Dogali in Abyssinia (Ethiopia)
1889	Italy claims protectorate over Abyssinia by Treaty of Ucciali
1896	Major defeat of Italian troops by Abyssinian forces at Adowa. Italy renounces claims to Tunis
1898	Bread riots in Milan suppressed with considerable loss of life. Franco-Italian tariff war ended by commercial treaty
1900	Assassination of King Umberto
1904	General strike in Italy, with violent incidents in Milan. Subsequent elections return a conservative majority
1911	Italy declares war on Turkey and annexes Libya
1912	Introduction of new electoral law by Giolitti
1914	Outbreak of First World War, in which Italy is initially neutral
1915	Italy enters First World War as ally of Britain and France
1919	March: Formation of first Fascist 'combat group' by Mussolini
	September: Seizure of Fiume by D'Annunzio
1921	October: Fascist 'March on Rome'
1922	October: Mussolini appointed Prime Minister

Risorgimento (Italian –
'Resurgence'): The name
given to the movement for
Italian liberation and
unification in the 19th
century. It was based upon
the assumption that Italy
was, in effect, recovering
the predominance that it
had enjoyed in the days of
the Roman Empire.

Piedmont: The former
Italian kingdom that had
led the causes of Italian
unification and resistance
to Austrian rule in Italy in
the mid-19th century.
Piedmont was one of the
prosperous northern
regions of Italy.

Idealists: People whose
beliefs and behaviour are
based on ideals.

ITALY in 1870 was Europe's youngest state, its unification only completed that year by the occupation of Rome. It had been brought together by a combination of forces, not always working towards the same goal. The greatest statesman of the *Risorgimento*, Camillo di Cavour, had been primarily concerned to consolidate and to expand the authority of the Kingdom of **Piedmont** in northern Italy and to eliminate the challenge that Austria posed to it in those parts. Others desired the creation of a united Italian state, but even these differed over the nature of that united state. **Idealists** such as Giuseppe Mazzini and Giuseppe Garibaldi worked for a radical state, directed by principles of popular sovereignty. Others were happy to accept the leadership of a conservative monarchy, and placed their trust in King Victor Emmanuel II of Piedmont. The two programmes came together in 1860 when, grasping the opportunity provided by the defeat of Austria in 1859, Garibaldi seized the southern territories of Sicily and Naples. Realising that the only alternatives now were to accept a radical southern republic, or to embrace the principle of full unification, Cavour spent the last months of his life ensuring that Piedmontese authority and Piedmontese institutions would predominate in the south. He ensured that it would not be swamped there by the radicalism of Garibaldi. As a result, Cavour's successors were faced with the complex problems of bringing modern nationhood and economic prosperity to a state whose superficial unity was based upon neither of these elements.

It is important to bear this background in mind when assessing the degree of success achieved by Italian governments between 1870 and 1943. Similarly, you are likely to gain an imperfect understanding of Italian Fascism if it is placed too much in the context of inter-war Europe, rather than that of pre-1914 Italy. Dominated by the administrations of Francesco Crispi and Giovanni Giolitti, Italian governments between 1870 and 1914 sought to modernise Italy by many of the conventional methods used by other European regimes at this time: industrialisation; foreign expansion; colonial policy. Giolitti seriously sought a broader, firmer base of parliamentary support as the basis of strength for his government. The impact of the First World War upon Italy was similar to that upon other European states: serious economic consequences for a national economy that had been quite unprepared for such strains in 1914. The conduct of the war also did much to discredit the regime, and the political ideals that had led Italy into such a conflict. What was unusual in the case of Italy was that these ideals were parliamentary and liberal, and it is a measure of the shallowness of their roots that such ideals should have been submerged in Italy, when they survived in post-war France or Britain. In Italy, however, the ineffectiveness of parliamentary politicians was blamed, with some justification, for the conduct of the war, and for Italy's failure to achieve the territorial gains for which it had entered the war in the first place. Here, as elsewhere in Europe, the threat of communism provided an added impetus towards the establishment of a political movement that offered a tempting mixture of economic security, social conservatism, and national self-fulfilment. It should not surprise us that Benito Mussolini's Fascist movement gained such a rapid and complete hold over the rival political forces. Parliamentary democracy was weak and unpopular in any case. The traditional ruling élites merely tolerated rather than valued it, and the Catholic Church had opposed it from the outset. By October 1922 Italy faced the prospect of a civil war between fascism and left wing groups such as socialists and communists. In these circumstances the King chose to side with the fascists. In October 1922 Mussolini was appointed prime minister of a coalition government. The fascists were in the minority. Would Mussolini be just another Italian prime minister who would govern for a short period of time or would he break the mould of Italian politics?

Italy's Prime Ministers, 1869–1943

J. Lanza	Dec. 1869 – July 1873	G. Saracco	June 1900 – Feb. 1901
M. Minghetti	July 1873 – March 1876	G. Zanardelli	Feb. 1901 – Nov. 1903
A. Depretis	March 1876 – March 1878	G. Giolitti	Nov. 1903 – March 1905
B. Cairoli	March – Dec. 1878	A. Fortis	March 1905 – Feb. 1906
A. Depretis	Dec. 1878 – July 1879	S. de Sonnino	Feb.–May 1906
B. Cairoli	July 1879 – May 1881	G. Giolitti	May 1906 – Dec. 1909
A. Depretis	May 1881 – August 1887	S. de Sonnino	Dec. 1909 – March 1910
F. Crispi	August 1887 – Feb. 1891	L. Luzzatti	March 1910 – March 1911
A. di Rudini	Feb. 1891 – May 1892	G. Giolitti	March 1911 – March 1914
J. Giolitti	May–Dec. 1893	A. Salandra	March 1914 – June 1916
F. Crispi	Dec. 1893 – March 1896	P. Boselli	June 1916 – Oct. 1917
A. di Rudini	March 1896 – June 1898	V. Orlando	Oct. 1917 – June 1919
L. Pelloux	June 1898 – June 1900	G. Giolitti	June 1919 – June 1920
		L. Faeta	June 1920 – Feb. 1922
		B. Mussolini	Feb. 1922 – July 1943

---

1. Which of the factors in the mind map are examples supporting the view that Italy was a weak state after 1870? Give reasons for your answer.

2. Which factors mentioned in the mind map are examples of Italian success?

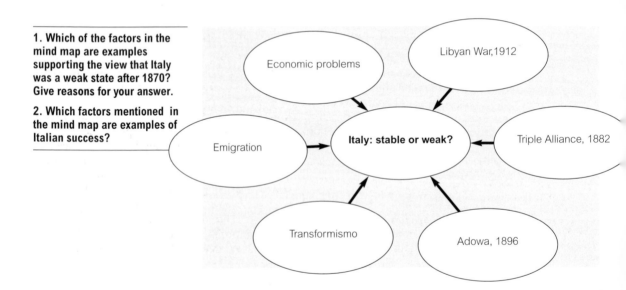

4.1 How strong was parliamentary government in Italy between 1871 and 1914?

The background and nature of Italian parliamentary government

Superficially, it might seem surprising that Fascism established itself so firmly in Italy, a state apparently founded throughout its 60 years' existence up to 1920 upon liberal parliamentary principles and upon the moderate concepts of constitutional monarchy. The fact becomes easier to understand when one analyses the historical background of Italian democracy, and appreciates the factors that distinguished it from other European varieties.

The Italian state and the Italian constitution at the end of the 19th century were direct results of the politics of the *Risorgimento*, the movement by which Italy was unified in the mid-century. Italy's constitution was, in effect, the limited constitution (*Il Statuto*) that had been granted in Piedmont in the course of the 1848 revolutions. Its strict qualifications, based upon property and upon literacy, limited the electorate in 1870 to 8% of adult males (2.2% of the total population). This left the Crown with extensive powers. The constitution specifically acknowledged the King as 'the supreme Head of State; he commands all the land and naval forces; he declares war, he makes treaties of peace, alliance, commerce, etc., informing parliament of them as soon as the interests and security of the State permit'. In support of the monarchy, the Italian army remained large and heavily financed, partly as a means of advertising Italy's 'great power' status, but also because of the high degree of internal unrest that characterised this stage of Italian history. A 'state of siege', involving martial law and the substitution of military courts for the normal civil courts, was declared on ten occasions between 1861 and 1922. 'Italy was not yet a peaceful enough country,' writes Martin Clark in *Modern Italy 1871–1982* (1984), 'to survive without periods of military law and military repression, [and] each military intervention lowered the prestige of the Crown and made national unity even more precarious.'

Parliamentary politics and 'Transformism'

In addition to, and perhaps as a result of, its limited powers, Italian parliamentary politics were characterised by a weak party system. Deputies represented the interests of their constituents, rather than the ideology of a political party, and were likely to lose their seats if they could not secure favours from ministers. Ministers had no firm basis of party loyalty to rely upon and were likely to lose office if they did not dispense favours to a sufficient number of deputies. Indeed, by 1892 Italy had experienced 28 different governments in its 32 years as a unified state. The result of such instability was '**Transformism**' (*traformismo*). The three longest-serving premiers of the period – Agostino Depretis, Francesco Crispi and Giovanni Giolitti – were all masters of the practice. Thus it eliminated true party spirit and ruled out any real clash of alternative party principles. It is easy to understand how parliamentary politics came to be regarded by many Italian observers as corrupt and self-interested, a far cry from the high principles that had motivated many of the heroes of the *Risorgimento*. All too often, it seemed, what was justified as a means to political stability

'Transformism' (*traformismo*): The practice first developed by Cavour of welding together large and unlikely coalitions in support of ministries. By granting favours to individuals or to the communities that they represented, ministers might 'transform' opponents into supporters and improve the prospects of their administration and of their legislative programmes.

Agostino Depretis (1813–1887)
A follower of Mazzini in his youth, Depretis later supported the form of Italian unity represented by Cavour and the Piedmontese monarchy. He entered the Italian parliament in 1873, and was Prime Minister on several occasions between 1876 and 1881. His administrations passed important reforms concerning education, taxation and the franchise, and engineered Italy's entry into the Triple Alliance (1882).

Francesco Crispi (1819–1901)
Active in revolt against the King of Naples in 1848, and subsequently in exile. A prominent member of Garibaldi's expedition to Sicily (1860) and an opponent of Piedmont's annexation of Sicily and Naples. He served as Minister of the Interior (1876 and 1877) and Prime Minister (1887–90, 1893–96). In foreign affairs his policy was pro-German, anti-French, and in favour of colonial expansion.

Giovanni Giolitti (1842–1928)
Minister of Finance under Crispi (1889–90). Minister of the Interior (1901–03). Prime Minister (1903–05, 1906–09, 1911–14). In his last years Giolitti was an opponent of Fascism, having failed to form an electoral alliance with Mussolini.

became, in Denis Mack Smith's words, 'a common refuge where they laid aside their internal quarrels and joined in parcelling out power and jobbery'.

Although this form of administration had its legislative successes, Italy remained a country of enormous social and economic problems. In many respects Giolitti, in particular, was a worthy successor to Cavour, the greatest politician of the *Risorgimento*. Cavour had brought about substantial improvements in the economic prosperity of Piedmont, but he had often done so by political means that would have seemed extremely dubious in France or in Great Britain. Giolitti's administrations could also point to important successes, including a range of laws for agricultural improvement (1897–1906) and an important new electoral law (1912). The rate of illiteracy – one of Italy's most profound problems – was reduced to 11% in the north, although it remained as high as 90% in parts of southern Italy. Such was the cost of 'Transformism'.

Even relatively successful and stable ministries made little effort to reform the major problems of southern Italy – agricultural backwardness, the influence of the great landowners, the power of the Mafia in Sicily – largely because of the political difficulties that such policies would have entailed. The southern provinces remained backward and poverty-stricken, with 90% of Sicilian army recruits rejected as medically unfit. The sociologist L. Franchetti described in 1902 how 'peasant risings, which usually lead to bloodshed, are characteristic and normal events in the public life of the south', which was 'without any middle class, even without workers who are above the poverty level and possess a rudimentary education'.

It is worth noting that the problems of the south also had an impact upon the development of the more prosperous north. Illiterate and unskilled, the southern peasant was difficult to employ in any industrial capacity, and was highly unlikely to serve as a consumer of the north's industrial produce. The product of 'Transformism' was, in short, partial and unsatisfactory.

The enemies of Italian democracy

Beyond the inherent weaknesses of the Italian parliamentary system, two major groups regarded the liberal state with almost unrelieved hostility. One was the growing force of socialism, stimulated by the industrial growth of the north in the late 1880s and the early 1890s, and to a lesser extent by the poverty of agricultural workers. By the eve of the First World War, the socialists were capturing 25% of electoral votes. As an alternative to liberalism before the war it was weakened by its constant divisions, and by the preference of many of its leaders for reform rather than revolution. Its many offshoots, such as the anarchists, the **syndicalists** and the early Communist Party, represented a substantial force in opposition to the whole basis of parliamentary government.

Syndicalists: Industrial workers belonging to the syndicalism movement which had as its objective the transfer of the means of production and distribution from their present owners to unions of workers for the benefit of the workers. The method generally favoured for this was the general strike.

Political tension was heightened in the 1890s by a bitter and protracted 'tariff war' with France. Protective tariffs adopted by France provoked Italian counter-measures, causing a reduction in Italian exports and ending many of the French loans that had recently helped to finance Italy's industrial expansion. Unemployment rose in northern industrial areas, and there were bread riots in Milan (May 1898). A railway strike in 1902 and a general strike in 1904 helped to increase the general sense of political tension. The plans of Luigi Pelloux's government in 1898 to introduce martial law and to govern by royal decree provided a foretaste of Fascist measures. The assassination of King Umberto in 1900 only added to the sense of crisis.

By this stage, however, socialism had over-played its hand, and the elections of 1904 saw a heavy defeat for the radical left. For much of the decade before the First World War, Italian governments underestimated this opposition from the left. Giolitti claimed in parliament that the socialists had 'put Marx in the attic' and believed that his new electoral law (1912) would provide a broad basis of support for his form of government. In effect, the law provided universal male suffrage for all over the age of 30, with the exception of illiterates who had avoided military service. He was wrong. At the national congress of the Italian socialist party in 1912, the radical left gained the upper hand. Among the younger generation of socialist leaders, such as Benito Mussolini, opposition to bourgeois parliamentary government became stronger than ever. The elections that took place in 1913 under the new electoral law left the foundations of Italian parliamentary government no more secure than they had ever been.

The second hostile force was the Catholic Church. On poor terms with Piedmont from the 1850s onwards, the Church's relations with united Italy were totally undermined by the Italian seizure of Rome in 1870. Deprived by the Franco–Prussian War of its main political allies – the French – the **Papacy** could do no more than protest and express hostility to all subsequent Italian governments. Until the turn of the century the Church instructed good Catholics to **boycott** elections, and scarcely any leading figure in national politics was a practising Catholic. When Pope Pius X officially relaxed this boycott in 1904, it was not out of any regard for the state, but from fear of the increasing influence of socialism. The Church, therefore, became the potential ally of the more conservative elements in the state. As such, it was equally likely to be an ally, active or passive, of the anti-Marxist forces that arose in the wake of the First World War.

In addition to these hostile elements, the government might also expect to encounter opposition from another source. In the years immediately before the First World War, parliamentary government increasingly came under attack from resurgent nationalism. Such emotions were fuelled by the conviction of many patriots that the work of unification remained incomplete. Such '**irredentism**' was provoked by failures in Italian colonial policy. The wounds caused by the defeat and humiliation at Adowa, in Abyssinia (1896), never really healed.

In the decade before 1914, Enrico Corradini stood at the head of a militant nationalist movement which roundly blamed the failures of Italian colonial and foreign policy upon the 'soft' influences of the parliamentary regime. He received influential support from one of Italy's most famous writers, Gabriele D'Annunzio, who advocated an assertive and chauvinistic foreign policy, preferably under a government with a single, all-powerful leader. The nationalist movement received great stimulus from the war of 1911–12 in which Italy secured Libya from Turkey, while the mismanagement and huge cost of the war went further to discredit the existing regime. The entry of Italy into the European war in 1915 naturally enhanced the influence of this movement to an extent unprecedented since the capture of Rome in 1870.

Papacy: The position, power and authority of the Pope.

Boycott: Refusing to have any dealings with someone. The origins of the word 'boycott' lie in the nationalist agitation in Ireland in the late 1870s. During the depression of that time tenants were frequently evicted and the land taken over by others. Frequently, those who took over the land from evicted tenants were treated with hostility and given no help. This fate befell Captain Boycott in County Mayo.

'**Irredentism**': The view of Italian nationalists that, despite the achievements of the *Risorgimento*, certain Italian territories – such as Nice, Savoy, Dalmatia and Ilyria – remained 'unredeemed' (*irredenta*) from foreign control, and should be added to the united Italian state.

---

1. What were the main causes of political tension in Italy in the years between 1871 and 1914?

2. Why was it so difficult to establish a stable parliamentary democracy in Italy in the 40 years after unification?

Gabriele D'Annunzio (1863–1938)
One of Italy's most prolific writers of the period, he turned to an active role in nationalist politics in the years before the First World War. He was a supporter of direct and heroic political action, in the tradition of Guiseppe Garibaldi (1807–1882). This culminated in his seizure of Fiume in the name of Italy (1919).

4.2 To what extent was the Italian economy modernised and strengthened between unification and the outbreak of the First World War?

The economic inheritance of the Kingdom of Italy

To a large extent, German unification was based upon previous economic growth and development, but this was not the case with Italy. The Italian economy in the 1870s remained predominantly agricultural, with more than 60% of the working population employed on the land. Wide variations existed between different regions in agricultural practice and in the prosperity that these produced, especially between the far north and the far south. The agrarian economy of the south continued to be dominated by the vast feudal estates of the nobility (*latifundia*). Often absent from their estates, these owners had little direct concern for productivity or innovation. Employment was seasonal, and poverty was the rule for most of the peasant labourers. Circumstances were usually more favourable in the more fertile north, yet even there productivity was low by the standards of western Europe. With some 40% of the crop consumed by the farmers themselves, even the domestic market was often insufficiently supplied. In industrial terms, too, Italy suffered from the limited nature of its resources. Italy's potential as an industrial and military power was limited by the fact that its iron and steel production was very low. Fuel supplies were limited, with coal still only 12% of Italy's imports in 1914. In the north, on the other hand, water power was abundant and permitted the development of electrical, chemical and textile production in the later years of the 19th century.

Political unification did not bring about any rapid improvement. The process of unification had resulted in an enormous government debt, and the first two decades of union coincided with an international economic slump. The northern regions benefited, to an extent, from their contact with the more prosperous economies of western Europe. The historian Martin Clark describes them as being brought 'into close and often brutal contact with the modern world'. However there was little prospect of greater investment or greater enterprise in the south. Successive governments intervened energetically, but with limited effect. Railway construction, in particular, was perceived as a priority. Historian S.B. Clough refers, in *The Economic History of Modern Italy* (1964), to 'an almost frantic effort on the part of the government to get railways built where they did not exist'. Important as these railways were, they were constructed a decade or more before any significant upturn took place in the Italian economy, and they cannot be regarded as a direct stimulus.

Steadily, too, the government abandoned the traditional free trade policies of the Cavour era. Major tariffs introduced in 1878 and 1887 transformed Italy into a protectionist state. 'Behind tariff walls,' Tom Kemp notes, in *Industrialisation in Nineteenth Century Europe* (1985), 'the state extended direct and indirect aid to the heavy industries which the nationalists associated with economic independence and political power.' Even so, by 1914, annual steel production was still less than a million tons, and coal production stood only at 11.5 million tons. Italian society in the decades after unification continued to demonstrate many of the familiar symptoms of widespread poverty. In 1881, over 38% of all Italian army conscripts were rejected on grounds of poor health, deformity or insufficient growth. Between 1884 and 1886, 50,000 deaths from cholera were recorded, 27,000 from typhoid in 1887, and 15,000 per year in the 1880s from malaria.

How important was industry in Italy by 1914?

Some historians have claimed that it was during the years 1896–1914 that Italy experienced its true economic revolution. The period saw the foundation of the *Banca d'Italia* (Bank of Italy) and a considerable upswing in industrial production, supported by improved economic conditions across Europe as a whole. Giolitti's governments hastened this process by increasing the number of government orders placed with Italian manufacturers, by taking Italian railways into government ownership, and by launching a further ambitious programme of railway building. In the 25 years before the outbreak of the First World War, national income rose by 50%, and industrial production rose to constitute 25% of total national output.

Italy also played an active part in the early development of the motor industry, particularly with the establishment of the Fiat company in 1899. The benefits of this development were felt exclusively in the north, where a triangle formed by Milan, Genoa and Turin possessed a substantial working population and a prosperous middle class. Strenuous government efforts in the decade before 1914 to encourage industrial development in the south foundered upon the familiar obstacles of unskilled labour, lack of local resources, and a backward system of communications.

A similar pattern is evident in Italian agriculture. With the introduction of protective tariffs, agricultural prices and production increased, from 3.6 million tons in the mid-1890s to 4.6 million in 1911–13, but these benefits were mainly limited to such northern regions as Piedmont, Lombardy and southern Veneto. In relative terms, the south slipped further behind, and served largely as a source of cheap labour. The relative inability of the Italian economy to absorb this labour was clearly demonstrated by the amount of emigration: by 1914, nearly 6 million Italians out of 41 million lived and worked abroad. It also seems that the economic growth evident around the turn of the century was running out of steam long before the coming of war in 1914. A rate of growth that had reached nearly 14% per year between 1896 and 1908 had declined to a mere 2% per year in the last years of peace.

By 1914 it was just possible to perceive Italy as a developed industrial power. Politically, especially in the foreign and colonial arenas, its leaders behaved as though it was already the equal of the other great powers. Yet Italy suffered from some distinct weaknesses. Its growth rate was uneven, and in decline by 1914. There was too great an emphasis upon heavy industry, and the inequality between the north and the south was as striking as ever. Poverty remained a serious and widespread problem. The Italian economy, like the economies of other states that had made a late start to the process of industrialisation – like that of Russia for instance – could be judged in two distinct ways in 1914. Some historians have stressed the progress that was made from unpromising origins. On the other hand, it was foolish to believe that Italy was truly the equal of the great industrial states of Europe, and that it could match them in such trials as the world war would provide. Many problems remained to be solved before Italy could play the role that its nationalist leaders designed and advocated for it.

1. In what respects had Italy modernised its industrial economy by 1914?

2. What evidence is there for and against the claim that Italy became a modern, industrialised state in the years between 1871 and 1914?

4.3 By what means and with what success did Italy seek great power status in the years 1870–1914?

In many respects the *Risorgimento* had proved to be a 'partial revolution'. The state that it produced was guaranteed neither security nor self-respect by a process of unification that had depended so heavily upon the actions of other European powers. The state of mind of Italian patriots in the early years of unity has been neatly summarised by Martin Clark: 'There was a general feeling of disillusionment in post-1870 Italy. Rome had been won, but ingloriously; the *Risorgimento* had succeeded, but after too many lost battles; Italy had a large army, but other Europeans did not take it seriously.'

Italian colonial ambitions

Italy's colonial policy in the late 19th century had much in common with that of France at the same period. Both were dictated by the realities of the country's status in European politics. Just as the alternative for France was 'revenge' against Germany, the call from Italian nationalists was for a continuation of unification, for a bid to gain such territories as the South Tyrol, Istria or Dalmatia, which still lay in Austrian hands. With the prospect of further French support declining, and with the consistent improvement in Austro–German relations, such an 'irredentist' policy was scarcely possible. Italian prestige would have to be sought elsewhere.

Italy's colonial ambitions centred upon Africa, and particularly upon territories in the north and east of that continent. Ten years of involvement in Ethiopia and Eritrea, however, brought little success. The occupation of the port of Massawa on the Red Sea (1885) was undermined by the massacre of 500 Italian troops at Dogali (1887). The succession of the Emperor Menelik (1888) seemed to bring a pro-Italian ruler to the Ethiopian throne, but Menelik's sympathy for Italian interests evaporated as those interests extended deeper into Ethiopia and as a protectorate was established over Eritrea. Although Italian politicians disagreed about the value of colonial policy, Crispi's administration clearly regarded colonial commitment as the best way to distract attention from internal political divisions. His decision to intensify campaigns in Ethiopia led to disaster and humiliation when an Italian force was heavily defeated by Menelik at Adowa (1 March 1896). It was the only example in the 19th century of an African state gaining a definitive victory over a would-be coloniser, and had a predictable impact upon nationalist feelings within Italy. The most direct political result was the resignation of Crispi.

Italy achieved only a little more success in North Africa. Attempts to establish influence over Tunisia, only a relatively short distance from Sicily, clashed directly with those of France. Lacking the diplomatic 'muscle' to compete effectively, Italy had acknowledged that region as part of the French 'sphere of influence' by 1881. There was some later compensation, however, in the form of an agreement (1902) whereby France and Italy recognised the respective interests of each state in Morocco and in Libya, nominally a Turkish possession. When France began to implement its claims to Morocco (1911), it was time for Italy to take similar action in Libya. Strong financial and nationalist interests were also at work in this initiative. At first, the Libyan campaign proved no easier than that in Abyssinia, but the outbreak of war in the Balkans put Turkey in an impossible position, and by the end of 1912 it had cut its losses, leaving Libya under Italian control.

Italy's European diplomacy

In terms of European diplomacy, Italy found itself in an ambiguous position, which guaranteed its security, but left it with little scope for the pursuit of European territorial ambitions. In the course of the *Risorgimento* the keystone of Piedmontese/Italian foreign policy had been friendship with Britain and France. After 1870, French friendship was of relatively little value in the light of France's weakness and isolation. Besides, many factors had arisen since 1859 to undermine the good relations between the states.

● The transfer of Nice and Savoy to France in 1860 was never fully accepted.

● French and Italian ambitions in the western Mediterranean were incompatible.

● It came as a great blow to Italian prestige when, in 1881, the French occupied Tunisia, where Italian settlers hugely outnumbered French.

1. Why did Italy remain neutral in the First World War between August 1914 and May 1915?

2. Why did Italy finally decide to join the Allies rather than the Central Powers? Explain your answer.

Happily, Italy found itself courted by other powers. Good relations with the new and powerful German state had begun with military co-operation in 1866, and Bismarck proved eager to maintain those relations, not least as a means of guaranteeing the isolation of France. As Germany improved its relations with Austria, Italy found it easier to mend its own relations with that traditional enemy. This was the logic behind the Triple Alliance that was concluded between the three states in May 1882.

Postcard depicting Italy as the umpire of the First World War. From left to right: Austria and Germany versus Belgium, Great Britain, France and Russia.

1. In what regions and for what reasons did Italy seek colonial possessions in the decades after 1914?

2. To what extent did Italian foreign policy between 1871 and 1914 achieve its objectives?

Yet Italian attitudes to the Triple Alliance remained ambiguous. Conservative politicians relished this identification with the monarchical governments of Germany and Austria, while nationalists regretted that the treaty made it harder to squeeze further territorial concessions out of Austria. Besides, Italy had relatively little need of the guarantees that the treaty provided against French aggression. With the resolution of Franco–Italian disputes over North Africa, and with the steady extension of Austrian influence in the Balkans, it became harder to see just what advantages Italy derived from the Triple Alliance. Although it remained the official basis of Italian diplomacy on the eve of the First World War, such factors had eroded Italy's enthusiasm and commitment. Thus, upon the outbreak of war in 1914, Italy not only refused to act upon the terms of the Triple Alliance, but concluded an agreement with France. Under its terms, Italy undertook to declare war on its allies in return for a guarantee that it would gain Trento, the South Tyrol, Trieste and Dalmatia at the end of the conflict. It was a remarkable piece of political opportunism and in the light of the military and diplomatic failures that followed, was likely to discredit the politicians who took such a gamble.

4.4 What factors contributed to the rise of Italian Fascism in the years after the First World War?

The birth of the Fascist movement

The immediate post-war period held considerable promise for an ambitious politician. The frustrations of the peace treaty, the economic difficulties that produced two million Italian unemployed by November 1919, and the subsequent disillusionment of many ex-servicemen, reduced the prestige of the liberal regime to a new low ebb. It was under these circumstances, in March 1919, that Benito Mussolini formed the first 'combat group' (*Fascio di combattimento*) in Milan. The name of the group, and of the movement, was derived from the *fascio*, the insignia of the *lictors* of ancient Rome. Initially, the programme proposed by these 'Fascists' showed the continuing influence of left-wing politics, and especially of French syndicalism. They proposed:

Fascio: A bundle of rods with an axe at its centre. It was a symbol of unity and strength.

Lictors: Officials in ancient Rome who accompanied and protected the magistrates of the city, and who bore the symbols of the magistrates' office.

- the abolition of the monarchy and the establishment of a republic;

- the decentralisation of government;

- the abolition of conscription;

- the closure of all banks and of the stock exchange;

- profit sharing and management participation by the workers;

- the seizure of Church lands.

For Mussolini, however, as Denis Mack Smith states, in *Mussolini* (1981), 'Fascism was not a system of immutable [unchanging] beliefs but a path to political power'. When the party only polled 4,795 votes in the Milan elections of November 1919, Fascist policy began a steady movement to the right.

Although the rise of Fascism in Italy had deeper and more complex causes than Benito Mussolini, his personality had a profound influence upon the form taken by the movement (see profile). Identified with the left wing of Italian socialism, Mussolini was a violent critic of parliamentary government, and of those socialists who sought parliamentary seats. His solutions to the social and economic problems of contemporary Italy were revolutionary, and he was vitriolic in his attacks upon socialists who sought change by moderate reform.

The outbreak of war brought about a radical change in Mussolini's political stance. By condemning Italian neutrality in a sensational editorial in

Mussolini with Blackshirt leaders on the March of Rome, 28 October 1922

Benito Mussolini (1883–1945)

Born (29 July 1883) the son of a blacksmith, near Forli in the Romagna. Mussolini's hostility towards bourgeois society may be traced to his hard childhood, and to the enthusiastic, republican socialism of his father. In his turbulent, violent personality as a young man may be seen the beginnings of the vigorous, often incoherent, gestures that later characterised so much of Fascist policy. The young Mussolini was expelled four times from his various schools for indiscipline and violence. His biographer, Denis Mack Smith, has concluded that the innate streak of violence in his character was of as great importance in his development as any of the political philosophers by whom he later claimed to have been influenced.

Failing to find satisfaction or success in his brief career as a teacher, Mussolini was soon set upon the road of political agitation, organisation and journalism. His success as editor of a provincial socialist journal (1909–12) led to national recognition and appointment to the editorship of Italy's primary socialist newspaper *Avanti!* (Forward!) in November 1912. Some of the future bases of Fascism can be discerned in his views during this period.

Mussolini was expelled from the socialist movement in 1914 for advocating Italian intervention in the First World War. In 1919, he founded the Fascist Movement, which was backed by many landowners and industrialists and by the heads of the army and police. He became Prime Minister (October 1922) as head of a coalition government. In 1925, he assumed dictatorial powers, and banned all opposition parties. His Blackshirt followers (see photo) were the forerunners of Hitler's Brownshirts. During the Second World War Mussolini's prestige was destroyed by defeats in Africa and Greece, the allied invasion of Sicily and discontent at home. He was compelled to resign (July 1943) by his own Fascist Grand Council. Mussolini was freed from prison by German parachutists two months later and set up a Fascist government in north Italy. He and his mistress, Clara Petacci, were captured while heading for the Swiss border, and shot.

Avanti! (18 October 1914), Mussolini not only flew in the face of accepted socialist policy, but effectively turned his back on the party for ever. His change of heart has been interpreted in a variety of fashions. His former socialist colleagues, in their sense of betrayal, brought charges of foreign bribery. Other critics have seen it as an acknowledgement that, with his recent election defeat in Forli (October 1913) and the collapse of the revolutionary 'Red Week' riots (June 1914), the political future of socialism seemed bleak. His biographer Christopher Hibbert has been more generous in his view (1962) that Mussolini was attracted to intervention in the war by the anticipation that it would bring nearer the revolutionary upheaval for which he hoped. Although Fascist historians later invented a number of heroic exploits for Mussolini, his military service seems to have been uneventful, apart from an injury received during a training exercise. When he returned to civilian life and journalism, the editorials of his new journal *Il Popolo d'Italia* (The Italian People) were distinguished by views easily recognisable as Fascism. Prominent among them were the demand that post-war Italy should be governed by those who had fought for the country, and the resentment that Italy should be cheated of such fruits of victory as Fiume (see below).

The nature of Fascist support

Squadristi: The paramilitary (see page 81) units used by the Fascist Party in Italy to terrorise political opponents.

From 1920, Fascist policy stressed the twin themes of nationalism and anti-Bolshevism. Fervent support for D'Annunzio in his spectacular, illegal seizure of the city of Fiume for Italy (September 1919) seemed almost to annex him to the Fascist cause. Meanwhile, the anti-communist violence of the Fascist action squads (*Squadristi*) and the new party line in favour of free enterprise went a long way towards reassuring the middle classes. The change of direction was a substantial success. Big business was eager to subsidise this valuable anti-communist force, and substantial contributions from such sources as the Fiat motor company, the Pirelli tyre company and the Italian Banking Association put the Fascists on a firmer financial footing than most of their rivals. By late 1921 the party claimed 320,000 members, of whom 18,000 were landowners, 14,000 were small-scale traders, and

4,000 were industrialists. However, many of the party's members were peasants (36,000) or members of the urban working classes (23,000) seeking a refuge from what they saw as the twin evils of capitalism and socialism.

The spectacular growth of this Fascist faction made it a natural candidate for a place in one of the government's 'Transformist' coalitions. Giolitti had already aided the growth of Fascism by turning a blind eye to the excesses of the *Squadristi* when, in May 1921, he accepted Mussolini's offer of an electoral pact. As part of a government alliance, the Fascists won 35 parliamentary seats in the elections of that year. This was a small start in a house of 535 seats, but it gave Mussolini and his fellow deputies a new authority, respectability and a valuable freedom from arrest.

What were Mussolini's tactics as leader of the Fascist movement?

It was neither probable nor desirable to many in the Fascist movement that they should come to power by these parliamentary means. Mussolini himself found his style of public speaking ill-suited to parliamentary debate, while other Fascist deputies showed their contempt for the institution by brandishing pistols in the chamber and assaulting socialist deputies.

In the event, the crisis in Italian politics continued to operate to the advantage of the Fascists. A general strike called by the socialists in August 1922 gave the *Squadristi* an opportunity to pose as the country's sole protection against the imminent 'red' threat. The strike, badly organised and ill led, collapsed within 24 hours, creating the impression that the nation had been saved while the liberal regime stood helplessly by. At the same time as formulating a plan for the seizure of strategic points in Milan and other major cities, and for a subsequent march on Rome, Mussolini sought to reassure influential sectors of Italian opinion of Fascism's regard for the monarchy and for economic liberalism.

The *coup d'état* began on 27 October 1922. In many cities, the active or passive support of local government guaranteed success, but it seemed unlikely that the 26,000 Fascists converging on Rome could succeed against the regular troops in their path. Success was, however, guaranteed by the surprising refusal of King Victor Emmanuel III to sign his Prime Minister's decree of martial law. Historians seeking to explain this fateful timidity have variously stressed the degree of pro-Fascist feeling in court circles, and the effect of veiled Fascist threats to replace the king with the Duke of Aosta. 'Temperamentally,' wrote Denis Mack Smith, the king 'was drawn to anyone who would take firm decisions and control domestic unrest.' Putting aside any doubts, Mussolini exploited his position of strength and had, by 29 October, received a royal summons to form a ministry as the youngest Prime Minister in Italian history.

The official historians of Fascism portrayed the events of October 1922 as a glorious national revolution. More recently, it has become fashionable to belittle the Fascist rising and to stress the surrender of the regime through panic, weakness or self-interest. The truth lies between the two extremes. The insurrection was, indeed, a bold stroke, a substantial risk by its leaders. It was carefully and intelligently prepared. On the other hand, it was resistible. Fascism owed its triumph ultimately, not to Fascists alone, but to the mass of conservatives, businessmen, army officers, traders and peasants who saw Mussolini as the alternative to anarchy.

1. In what ways and for what reasons did Mussolini's political views become more right wing between 1910 and the early 1920s?

2. Which sections of the Italian population were most attracted to Fascism in the early 1920s, and for what reasons?

By what means and with what success did the Fascist dictatorship establish its control over the Italian state?

The dismantling of parliamentarianism
It was never likely that the Fascist leadership would be content merely to

capture the machinery of the liberal state. After an initially conciliatory attitude to other non-socialist parties, the first years in power were dedicated to the steady destruction of parliamentarianism in Italy. The success of the party's *Squadristi* in the early years of the movement was such that Mussolini now transformed them (December 1922) into an official **paramilitary** body called the Volunteer Militia for National Security. Their wholesale use of violence and intimidation was to be a prominent feature of Italian elections in the 1920s.

Paramilitary: An organisation which is similar to an army but is not the official army of the country. This term is often used to describe guerrilla outfits.

The new Prime Minister also had more subtle means at his disposal. A new electoral law was drafted by G. Acerbo (July 1923) which aimed to transform Fascism's minority status. It proposed that any party gaining more votes than any of its rivals, providing that it gained at least 25% of the total, would be entitled to two-thirds of the seats in the assembly. This, it was claimed, was in the interests of political stability. It should be noted that this law, like others in the early days of Mussolini's power, was passed with the help of liberal votes.

This form of parliamentary government limped on for five years, until a further electoral law (September 1928) decreed that the whole composition of parliament should be determined by the Fascist Grand Council, headed by Mussolini. This body would formulate a list of 400 nominees, which the electorate would be invited to accept or reject *en masse*. Given the means of intimidation in the government's hands, it is perhaps surprising that as many as 136,000 voters rejected the list in 1929. By 1934, however, the number of rejections had fallen to 15,000.

Matteotti's murder and the 'Aventine Secession'

The Acerbo electoral law and the violence of the 1924 elections also began the decisive clash with the Fascist Party's major rivals, the socialists. A socialist deputy, Giacomo Matteotti, showed great courage in his open defiance and criticism of Fascist methods. This led to his kidnap and subsequent murder by Fascist thugs. Whether or not Mussolini had directly encouraged or ordered the crime, he clearly bore the moral responsibility for it, and his political position became extremely vulnerable. Two factors aided his survival. Once again, the political tactics of the socialists were naïve. Their reaction to the death of Matteotti was to leave parliament in protest. This action became known as the 'Aventine Secession', in remembrance of an incident in ancient Roman history. Their eloquent gesture merely left the Fascists in fuller control. Secondly, King Victor Emmanuel, the only man with the constitutional power to dismiss Mussolini, once again shirked a hard decision and accepted the argument of force.

Initially shaken by the Matteotti crisis, Mussolini now seemed to exploit the new-found strength of his position. The historian F.W. Deakin has stressed, in *The Brutal Friendship* (1962), the important role in this played by subordinates. Of special importance was the work of the new party secretary, Roberto Farinacci, in overhauling and centralising the party machinery for the tasks of national government. The first months of 1925 saw a miniature 'reign of terror' characterised by house searches, closures of hostile newspapers, harassment of political opponents and constant attacks upon freedom of association and of speech. In November, a plot against Mussolini's life by a former socialist deputy, Zaniboni, provided the pretext for the official suppression of the socialist party. A series of decrees to strengthen the powers of provincial Fascist officers, a formal decree (October 1926) banning all other political parties and the formation (September 1926) of a secret police force, the OVRA, completed the apparatus of political dictatorship.

Roberto Farinacci (1892–1945)
Originally a nationalist journalist and an agitator in favour of Italian intervention in the First World War. Secretary General of the Fascist Party (1925–26). Member of the Fascist Grand Council (1935–43). Arrested and executed by partisans at the end of the Second World War.

1. What steps did the Fascists take in the 1920s to weaken the authority of parliament in the Italian political system?

2. What events transformed the Fascists so rapidly from an extreme political faction to a party of government?

4.5 How did Mussolini become dictator of Italy?
A CASE STUDY IN HISTORICAL INTERPRETATION

■ Did he rise to power because of the weakness of the Liberal political system?

■ Was he merely an opportunist in his rise to power?

■ How did he consolidate his hold on power from 1922 to 1925?

Framework of Events

1919	March: Mussolini founded *Fasci di Combattimento* ('Combat Group')
	2–3 November: Fascists heavily defeated in national elections
1919–20	*Bienno Rosso* ('The Two Red Years') created industrial unrest in north Italy
1920	Breakthrough for Fascists with rise of agrarian fascism
1921	Fascists win 35 seats in national elections
	November: Fascist Party (PNF) created
1922	February: Facta became Italian Prime Minister
	Pope Pius XI elected
	August: Failure of general strike broken by Fascists
	27–8 October: Fascist March on Rome
	29 October: Mussolini offered post of Prime Minister
	16 November: Mussolini given extraordinary powers by parliament
	December: Creation of National Fascist Militia (MSVN)
1923	November: Acerbo Election Law passed
1924	April: Fascists win landslide victory in national elections
	June: Murder of Socialist deputy, Matteotti, by Fascist thugs
	Aventine Secession
1925	January: Mussolini declared his dictatorship

O N October 29 1922, King Victor Emmanuel III offered Mussolini the post of Prime Minister. Borrowing a frock coat, Mussolini looked just like his liberal predecessors. However, his rise to political power was both swift and remarkable. Having acquired this power, Mussolini was determined not to give it up. As a result he became both the youngest and longest-serving Italian Prime Minister of the twentieth century. How was this achieved? Was it deep-rooted problems in Italy's political system, brought to the fore by the social, economic and political crises of the First World War, that led to Mussolini's rise to power? Or, was Mussolini, through his own abilities and the support of a few figures, able to gain control of Italy and force it along a completely new political path?

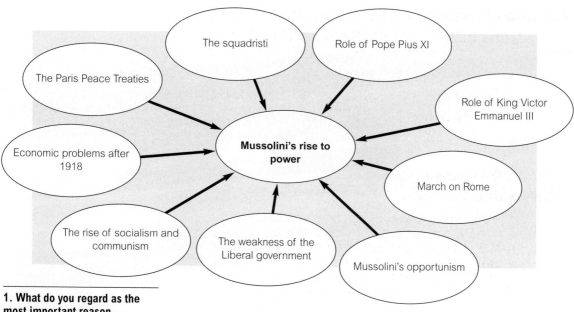

1. What do you regard as the most important reason explaining Mussolini's rise to power? Explain your answer.

2. Which of the factors in the mind map can be linked? For instance, economic problems after 1918 and the rise of socialism and communism are linked. Can you find any other links?

Did Mussolini rise to power because of the weakness of the Liberal political system?

Italy's constitution at the time of Mussolini's rise to power was based upon the limited model that had been granted at the time of Italy's unification in 1861. Italy was a constitutional monarchy, with King Victor Emannuel III recognised as Head of State, which gave him extensive powers. The government, which comprised two chambers, was chosen by the national parliament. Of the two chambers, the King nominated the senate's members, while the Chamber of Deputies was elected. However, the proportion of Italians engaged in national politics was very small. Before 1912, approximately 2.2 per cent of the population had the right to vote. This later rose to 8.6 million, or 24 per cent of the adult population, when the vote was then extended to all male literates over 21 years, or illiterates who had completed over 30 years of military service. Rome's incorporation into the Kingdom of Italy caused Pope Pius IX to lose his own independent territory, which led him to instruct Catholics not to participate in Italian politics. Since the vast majority of Italians were Catholics, this had a profound effect on the political system. The political nation really comprised only a small elite of middle-class politicians who shared political power with the King.

By 1892, Italy had experienced 28 governments in its 32 years as a unified state. Liberal politicians practiced 'transformism' in order to ensure political stability. However, rather than involving a wide cross-section of political opinion in government, it merely highlighted the rivalry between senior Liberal politicians. It is easy to see, therefore, how the Italian population viewed the Liberal political system as corrupt.

Antonio Salandra (1853–1931)

Prime Minister from March 1914 to June 1916, he was the chief architect of Italy's entry into the First World War. He was a lawyer and right-wing Liberal, and a deputy from 1886 to 1928. He attempted to create a Liberal-Nationalist coalition during Facta's premiership, and to form a coalition government on 27–28 October, which would include the Fascists. He cooperated with the Fascists until Mussolini's speech of 3 January 1925, announcing a dictatorship.

The Italian political system was further weakened when on 24 May 1915 Prime Minister Antonio Salandra, with the support of the King, entered Italy into the First World War on the side of the Allies without consulting either parliament or the Italian people. British historian, Denis Mack Smith, in *Italy: A Modern History* (1967), concludes that Mussolini's Fascism was a political system that naturally developed from a system that had failed to involve the Italian population.

The impact of the First World War

Italy's involvement in the First World War had an immense impact: 600 000 soldiers died; over 400 000 were captured; and three million served in the armed forces. Two battles were of great significance to Italy: Caporetto and Vittorio Veneto. In October 1917, the Italians suffered a major defeat by Austro-German forces at Caporetto, which almost forced Italy out of the war. However, Caporetto resulted in major changes in government and the army, and created a national mood of patriotism. In September 1918, at Vittorio Veneto, Italy won a major victory against the Austro-Hungarian army. It gave Italians the belief that they would be a major beneficiary of the peace treaties after the war. Unfortunately, while they had hoped for large parts of the Dalmatian coast, including the port of Fiume, at the **Paris Peace Conference** Italy received only the Trentino and Trieste. The Peace Treaties were seen as a humiliation for Italy, creating the idea of a 'mutilated victory'.

The war also placed a great strain on the Italian economy. The cost of living rose 300 per cent, and at the end of the war two million servicemen were demobilised, creating a major unemployment problem. By November 1918, millions of Italians had been involved in a national struggle like never before.

In 1919, a new electoral law created universal suffrage. For the first time the Italian masses had the opportunity to participate in national politics. Also in 1919, Pope Benedict XV (1914–22) allowed the creation of the Catholic Political Party (the Popolari or PPI). Thus from 1919, Italy entered the realm of mass politics. The old liberal elite found it very difficult to adjust. In the November 1919 elections they faced the new challenge of the PSI and PPI. Both parties did exceptionally well at the expense of the Liberals.

In *The Rise of Fascism* (1967), historian F. L. Carsten claims that Fascism did not exist before the First World War but rather it was this great social, economic and political upheaval that created the conditions for it to arise. Mussolini was able to exploit these conditions to gain political power.

Paris Peace Conference (1919–20): The assembly held after the First World War during which the League of Nations was set up and the peace agreements between the Allied and Central Powers were worked out. These proceedings were dominated by Britain, France, Italy, Japan and the USA, although 32 nations took part.

Mussolini assumes a characteristic pose as he speaks to an audience in Italy in 1934.

Was Mussolini merely an opportunist in his rise to power?

Historians Denis Mack Smith and Renzo de Felice regard Mussolini's personality as being central in his rise to power. He is viewed as an opportunist, exploiting situations and reacting to circumstances in order to gain power.

In March 1919, Mussolini had founded the *Fasci di Combattimento*, whose programme was anti-clerical, anti-monarchist, nationalist and in favour of social reform. However, at this time, Italy was suffering from a severe post-war social and economic crisis, which successive Italian governments seemed incapable of dealing with. In 1919, unemployment reached two million. The wholesale price index that had been 100 in 1913 had risen to 412.9 by the end of the war in 1918, and to 590.7 by 1920. The value of shares halved in the same period. The **lira** fell from 30 to the pound in March 1919, to 100 to the pound by December 1920. Membership of socialist trade unions rose from 250000 in 1918, to 1.2 million by 1920. This resulted in two years of social unrest (1919/20), which were associated with trade union strikes and civil unrest. This period was termed *Bienno Rosso* ('Two Red Years').

Mussolini exploited the failure of successive Italian governments to deal with the post-war crisis. An example of this was Gabriele D'Annunzio's occupation of Fiume in September 1919. War hero D'Annunzio managed to achieve something that the Italian government

Lira: the italian currency prior to the introduction of the Euro in January 2001.

Italian Prime Ministers in office

Paolo Boselli	June 1916 – Oct. 1917	1 years 4 months
Vittorio Orlando	Oct. 1917 – June 1919	1 year 7 months
Francesco Nitti	June 1919 – June 1920	1 year
Giovanni Giolitti	June 1920 – July 1921	1 year 1 month
Ivanoe Bonomi	July 1921 – Feb. 1922	7 months
Luigi Facta	Feb. 1922 – Oct. 1922	8 months
Benito Mussolini	Oct. 1922 – July 1943	20 years 9 months

Treaty of London (1915): a treaty between the Allies and Italy. It promised Italy territory from Austria-Hungary, including the Trentino and Trieste. It also promised the modern-day coastline of Slovenia and Croatia, known as Dalmatia.

had failed to do in 1918: acquire territory promised to Italy by the **Treaty of London**, and which they failed to receive at the Paris Peace Conference, creating their 'mutilated victory'. For 14 months D'Annunzio created a corporate state. He had his supporters dressed in black shirts and used the traditional Roman salute. Only after considerable international pressure did the Italian government send troops to expel D'Annunzio. In *Modern Italy* (1984), historian Martin Clark states that 'D'Annunzio had proven that the Italian state was weak, that the army could be disloyal and had pioneered a new style of mass politics'. Mussolini quickly had his Fascist *Squadristi* ('Squad') adopt the traditional Roman salute and dress in black shirts, capitalising on D'Annunzio's achievement.

Fascist policy, however, was unpopular, and in the elections of November 1919 they failed to win any seats. Although the PSI won 156 seats, while the newly formed PPI won 107, it proved to be a disaster for all government parties. Mussolini reacted by simply changing the party programme.

Indeed the fragmented nature of the Fascist movement in 1919/20 actually helped Mussolini in his quest for power. Fascist groups with a range of political opinions, from radical to conservative, started to appear spontaneously across industrial areas in northern and central Italy. Fascist *Ras* leaders of these groups possessed considerable political power. Mussolini managed to hold this disparate movement together by keeping the party programme flexible, and altering policy to suit specific situations. His newspaper, *Il Popolo d'Italia*, became a great tool through which to get his views to the Italian public. He was also an exceptional public speaker and a nationally known figure, all of which he exploited.

Ras: Ethiopian term for local chieftain, which was used to describe local bosses of Fascist movements.

The climax of *Bienno Rosso* came in August 1920 with the occupation of factories by socialist trade unionists across northern Italy. At this time, however, the Fascist movement also had a breakthrough as it began to develop support in rural areas. By 1920, *Federterra* ('socialist peasant leagues') had arisen, which led to the growth of anti-socialist sentiment in both urban and rural areas of Italy, which the Fascists exploited. Mussolini, therefore, changed the party policy, adopting a more conservative, nationalist and anti-socialist programme, which provided a more attractive alternative to the social and political chaos facing Italy. A mixture of legitimate political activity and illegal violence against political opponents enabled him to implement these changes. Mussolini's Fascist *Squadristi* terrorised opponents by attacking trade union halls and the offices of the PSI and *Avanti!*. Arson and murder were the hallmarks of Fascist violence and this 'twin track' approach of legal and illegal methods was a consistent feature of Mussolini's method of operation, even after he acquired political power.

Giovanni Giolitti's government proved incapable of solving the growing social and economic problems, which led him to call a general election in May 1921. Giolitti had hoped to see a major fall in PSI support. However, the PSI still managed to return 122 deputies. With the PPI's refusal to serve under Giolitti, a new Prime Minister, Francesco Nitti, took office. This election was important for Mussolini. The Fascists received seven per cent of the vote, acquiring 35 seats, including one for Mussolini. As a deputy, Mussolini could no longer be arrested for any association with violence. This was particularly crucial for a court case in which he was claimed to have planned to violently overthrow the government. To give his government a broader base, Giolitti had hoped to include the Fascists – Mussolini refused. From 1921 to October 1922, successive Liberal politicians attempted to co-opt the support of Mussolini, which gave the Fascists obvious respectability. Mussolini's skill in this situation was in refusing to accept any post other than Prime Minister.

Roberto Farinacci (1892–1945)
A *Ras* of Cremona, he was one of the original Fascists from the meeting in Milan on March 23 1919. In the summer of 1922 he was appointed Consul General of the Fascist militia. From 1925/6 he was secretary to the PNF and was responsible for limiting the power of the press and the 'fascistisation' of the civil service. He was a member of the Fascist Grand Council from 1933, and fought in the Ethiopian War in the air force. He led the anti-Semitic campaign from 1938 against the Jews, and was executed by Italian partisans on 28 April 1945.

In August 1921, Mussolini signed a pact of pacification with the PSI to bring mutual attacks of violence to an end, which caused a temporary crisis within the Fascist movement. Three of the most important local *Ras*, Dino Grandi, Italo Balbo and Roberto Farinacci, refused to accept it. In an attempt to outflank his *Ras* opponents, Mussolini resigned briefly as *Il Duce*. He correctly calculated that without his national leadership, the movement would fragment. At a congress of urban Fascists, later in August, Mussolini admitted that he made a mistake in signing the pact, and through his great oratorical skill he won back the support of the rank and file, and the leadership. The congress marked the final transformation of the Fascists into a movement that was clearly anti-socialist and in favour of free enterprise capitalism.

Indeed, by 1921, Fascism had firmly established itself across northern and central Italy. On 9 November, Mussolini took the step of uniting these disparate Fascist movements as the Fascist Party (PNF). His reputation and charisma enabled him to transform Fascism from a nationalist alternative to socialism, into a nationalist, anti-socialist defender of Italy's law and order. Liberal politicians such as Giolitti believed that Fascist violence was merely a sign of the times rather than a permanent characteristic of the party programme. However, Fascist acts of violence enabled Mussolini to ensure that Italy remained ungovernable. He continued to support violence against political opponents while promoting Fascism as a national movement that could bring order to Italy. Denis Mack Smith, in *Mussolini* (1981), claims that: 'Fascism was not a system of immutable (unchanging) beliefs but a path to power'. When Mussolini's policies didn't gain him power, he simply changed them.

Pyschological warfare: The March on Rome

Luigi Facta (1861–1930)
Prime Minister from February to October 1922, deputy from 1892 to 1924, and lawyer by profession, he served as a minister in several governments from 1903. His government failed to contain rising political violence between Fascists and Socialists.

The appointment of Luigi Facta as Prime Minister in February 1922 greatly aided Mussolini in his quest for power. Denis Mack Smith describes Facta as 'a negligible politician' who was chosen because the other major Liberal politicians (Giolitti, Salandra and Orlando) were too jealous of each other. As the last Liberal Prime Minister of Italy, Facta seemed incapable of dealing with political violence between Fascists and Socialists. A contemporary comment on the Prime Minister was that he should be called 'verba' not 'facta' because he talked (verba) and never acted (facta).

In February, at the time of the general election, the Alliance of Labour was created from the socialist trade unions. In August, it organised a 24-hour general strike, which the Fascists helped to break up through violence. The Facta government was unable to deal with the situation.

Mussolini used the psychological threat of violence and civil war to win power. On 24 October, a mass meeting of Fascists was held in Naples.

Mussolini leading the March on Rome on 28 October 1922.

Mussolini declared that 'either they let us govern or we will seize power by marching on Rome'. By the night of 27 October, Fascists were gathering at four points around Rome (Perugia, Civita Vecchia, Monterotondo and Tivoli) ready to march on the capital. On the night of 27 to 28 October, Fascist squads occupied telephone exchanges and government offices across northern Italy. At 2:00 a.m. on the morning of 28 October, Facta acted. He asked for the King to impose martial law and send in the army to stop the Fascists. The King agreed. However, by 9:00 a.m. the King had changed his mind and refused to impose martial law. Facta resigned. The King then called on Salandra to form a coalition government with the Fascists. Mussolini refused and in his newspaper *Il Popolo d'Italia* declared: 'fascism would not abuse its victory. Let that be clear to all. Fascism wants power and will have it.'. On the advice of Giolitti, the King invited Mussolini to be Prime Minister on 29 October.

The role of the King and Liberal politicians

Mussolini became Italian Prime Minister at the head of a broad coalition government of the centre and right of Italian politics. At the critical moment, in October 1922, he had been greatly assisted in his quest for

---

Mussolini's First Government, October 1922

Mussolini (Fascist)	Prime Minister, Minister of the Interior, Foreign Minister
General Armando Diaz (Non-Party)	Minister of War
Federzoni (Nationalist)	Minister of Colonies
Oviglio (Fascist)	Minister of Justice
De Stefani (Fascist)	Minister of Finance
Tangorra (PPI)	Minister of Treasury
Gentile (Nationalist)	Minister of Education
Carnazza (Democrat)	Minister of Public Works
D'Araso (Liberal)	Minister of Agriculture
Rossi (Democrat)	Minister of Industry and Commerce
Cavazonni (PPI)	Minister of Labour and Social Welfare
De Cesare (Democrat)	Minister of Posts and Telegraph
Giurati (Fascist)	Minister of Liberated Provinces

power by the King. Why did the King change his mind about introducing martial law?

In *Mussolini* (1964), historian Sir Ivone Kirkpatrick argues that the King had been visited in the night by generals Diaz and Pecori Giraldi, who had insisted that the army would do its duty under martial law but stressed that he would be 'well not to put it (the army) to the test.' Alan Cassels, in *Fascist Italy* (1982), believes that the King was persuaded by Fascist sympathisers at the Court, and was also threatened with the idea that he might be replaced as King by his brother the Duke D'Aosta, who was a Fascist sympathiser. Denis Mack Smith asserts that Giolitti advised the King to choose Mussolini, a view supported by R. J. B. Bosworth, who claims:

'the main politicians eyed each other but could not unite. Salandra, Orlando and Giolitti, each awaited his own return to the Prime Ministership, but each indicated a preference that the post be entrusted to the young Mussolini rather than to a hated old rival.'

Finally, the King, receiving reports of the March on Rome, feared a civil war in which only the socialists or communists would benefit. In this sense he was partly duped. There were fewer than 30,000 Fascist militia, and these were poorly armed and had little food. Where the army had already begun to occupy public buildings, they had received little opposition from Fascists. In the end only 12 people died in the March on Rome, and many of these deaths were due to private vendettas. Mussolini's 'twin track' approach of acting like a legitimate politician while also using violent, non-parliamentary methods had been successful.

How did Mussolini consolidate his hold on power from 1922 to 1925?

Although Mussolini was Italian Prime Minister from October 1922, he still had very limited power. The PNF were a minority in the coalition government with only a small number of seats in the Chamber of Deputies and no representation in the Upper House, the senate. Mussolini could also still be sacked by the King. However, within just over two years Mussolini was confident enough to declare himself dictator.

There were many factors that helped Mussolini to consolidate his hold on power and declare his dictatorship. One factor was the appointment of Pope Pius XI, an overt anti-communist who, unlike his predecessor, felt that Catholics should not be heavily involved in politics. Sir Odo Russell, British Minister to the **Vatican**, outlined how 'Pius XI wished to withdraw the Church as far as possible from politics, so that Catholics may unite on a religious and moral basis.' As a result, the Pope was instrumental in getting the leader of the PPI, a Sicilian priest called Dom Luigi Sturzo, to resign on 10 July 1923, which meant that the Catholic PPI no longer proved a threat to Mussolini and the PNF.

Another factor was Mussolini's skill in acquiring support from the Catholic Church. He ordered religious instruction in all state-run schools and banned obscene publications and the use of contraceptives. Finally, he increased the salaries of priests and bishops, which were paid out of the public purse.

Even after becoming Prime Minister, Mussolini was still aided by the support, real or tacit, of Liberal politicians, which enabled him further to consolidate his power. On 16 November he addressed parliament, requesting extraordinary powers as Prime Minister in order to deal with the political and economic crisis. He advocated a policy that would end

Pope Pius XI (1922–39)
He was elected the same month as Facta became Prime Minister, February 1922. Born Achille Ratti, he had been Apostolic Visitor to Poland in 1918. He had witnessed, at first hand, the Communist invasion of Poland in the Russo-Polish War. From that moment on he had an acute dislike of communism.

Vatican: the headquarters of the Roman Catholic Church based in Rome.

Fascist Violence: An Example

'These raids were usually done with either the support of the police or with police knowledge. On 23 January 1921, Balbo for the first time led Fascists in the city of Ferrara on a raid into the countryside, and followed it up with similar raids in February and March. They marched into villages within a twenty-mile radius of Ferrara, beating up Socialists, occasionally killing them, and burning socialist newspaper offices, meeting places, and local party headquarters. Sometimes they merely harassed Socialists, shouting obscenities to them in the street and driving close to them on their motor cycles.'

From *Mussolini* by Jasper Ridley, 1997

Lausanne Conference (1923): the final peace settlement between Turkey and the Allies after the Second World War. Turkey surrendered all claim to former territories of the Ottoman Empire occupied by non-Turks. Italy kept the Dodecanese Islands.

League of Nations (1920): an international organisation created after the First World War in order to preserve the peace and settle disputes by discussion and agreement. Based on the idea of collective security, it had limited influence because its only weapon against wayward members was sanctions, and it failed to prevent aggression among member states. The USA never joined and the USSR only joined the League in 1934. Japan, Germany and Italy left the League in the 1930s.

Gerrymander: deliberately altering the boundaries of election districts to ensure the election of supporters.

political violence, instil national discipline and create a balanced budget. Mussolini was supported in his request by five former Prime Ministers; Nitti alone refused. With only five abstentions, only 26 senators out of 398 voted against Mussolini.

Another important factor was the merger between the PNF and the Nationalists in February 1923. To cement this merger, Mussolini emphasised his role as the national saviour of Italy in foreign affairs. He highlighted his attendance at the **Lausanne Conference**, even though he attended for only two days. His most significant foreign policy adventure, however, was the Corfu Incident. In August 1923 an Italian general, Tellini, was murdered on the Greek island of Corfu. Mussolini used the event to militarily occupy Corfu. He acted in defiance of the **League of Nations**, having already broken part of the peace treaties of 1919/20. Eventually, he was forced to withdraw, not by the League, but by the Conference of Ambassadors of European States. However, the Greeks paid the Italians 50 million lira in compensation. The Corfu Incident won Mussolini considerable praise at home as a man who defied the peace treaties that had created the 'mutilated victory' of 1919/20.

Mussolini also continued to use violence and intimidation to consolidate his political power. In December 1922 he turned the Fascist militia into Italy's national militia (MSVN), which acted as a political police force. During 1923 three opposition deputies were murdered and fifty physically attacked. Fascist violence reached its pinnacle during the elections of April 1924. To ensure his dominance over parliament Mussolini had passed the Acerbo Law in July 1923, which changed the electoral system so that any political party obtaining 25 per cent of the vote received 66 per cent of the seats in the Chamber. During the election campaign the MSVN attacked opposition meetings and supporters and destroyed their offices. Mussolini also **gerrymandered** electoral boundaries. As a result, the PNF received 374 seats against the opposition's 180 seats, mainly PSI and Communists. Throughout the campaign, Mussolini attempted to give the impression that he was unaware of the excesses of Fascist violence. However, there is evidence that he orchestrated much of what occurred. One incident almost cost him his position as Prime Minister: the murder of Socialist deputy, Giacomo Matteotti.

The Matteotti Affair (1924)

Giacomo Matteotti was the foremost opponent of Mussolini, who made outspoken attacks on Fascist violence. On 10 June 1924, he was murdered by a Fascist gang known as the Ceka (after the Soviet Terror Police), which was led by Dumini and Volpi. On the following day, Mussolini publically expressed his innocence in the affair. Italian historian Renzo de Felice claims that the murder took place without Mussolini's knowledge, although there is sufficient evidence to suggest that he knew. The Ceka had acted on the advice of two leading PNF members, Cesare Rossi and Filippo Marinelli, both close associates of Mussolini. Also, under Mussolini's orders, the Chamber of Deputies were prevented from meeting to discuss the affair. As a result, the PSI, PPI, Communists and many Liberal deputies withdrew from parliament in what was termed the **Aventine Secession**.

Aventine Secession: after the actions of politicians in Ancient Rome who went to the Aventine hill outside Rome to express their opposition to policy.

Mussolini survived the Matteotti affair for a number of reasons. First, the Pope disassociated himself from the actions of the PPI. Secondly, opposition was controlled through a programme of intimidation by the MSVN, which led to the withdrawal of deputies who opposed Mussolini, thus making it easier for him to deal with parliament. Therefore, on 24 June, only 21 out of 398 senators voted against Mussolini over the affair. Thirdly, Mussolini could have been dismissed by the King, who refused to act. Finally, on 3 January 1925, in front of a parliament packed with his supporters, Mussolini announced that he took full responsibility for the Matteotti affair. Mussolini's survival ultimately depended on the support of the senate, the King, the Pope and the Italian people. He had achieved his ambition of becoming dictator and had ensured that once in power he had no intention of leaving it.

Source-based questions: How did he become dictator of Italy?

1. Read the following extract and answer the question.

Mussolini becomes Prime Minister

'Lacking as he did any experience of government, Mussolini was remarkably undaunted by the task confronting him, and the fact testifies to his ability and self-confidence. All his new ministers, except one taken from Facta's government, were equally inexperienced. At his first cabinet meeting he laid down his general policy-pacification, national discipline and budget economics. Many fascists were expecting him to discard the constitution and establish armed rule, but whatever he said to the contrary, he knew that he was in power not as a result of revolution, but following a series of compromises with the King and representatives of the former liberal regime.'

(from Denis Mack Smith's *Mussolini*, Weidenfeld and Nicolson, 1981)

Using the extract above, and information from this section, how far was it true to say that in October 1922, Mussolini was given power rather than seizing it?

2. What do you regard as the most important reason why Mussolini was able to become dictator of Italy by 1925?

Further Reading

Texts designed for AS and A2 Level students

Italy: Liberalism and Fascism by Mark Robson (Hodder & Stoughton, Access to History series, 2000)

Mussolini and Fascist Italy by Martin Blinkhorn (Routledge, Lancaster Pamphlets, 1984)

Fascist Italy by John Hite and Chris Hinton (John Murray, Schools History Project, 1998)

More advanced reading

Mussolini by Denis Mack Smith (Weidenfeld & Nicolson, 1981)

Mussolini's Roman Empire by Denis Mack Smith (Penguin, 1977)

Modern Italy 1871–1982 by Martin Clark (Longman, History of Italy series, 1984)

Italian Foreign Policy 1870–1940 by C.J. Lowe and F. Marzari (Routledge & Kegan Paul, 1975)

5 Mussolini's Italy, 1922–1943

Key Issues

- How and why did Italy make the transition from democracy to Fascism between 1922 and 1925?

- What was the impact of Fascist rule upon Italian politics and society between 1922 and 1943?

- How successful was Mussolini's foreign and imperial policy?

5.1 Did the Fascist regime achieve a political revolution in Italy?

5.2 What was the impact of Fascism upon Italian culture, society and the economy?

5.3 Historical Interpretation: Was Mussolini's Italy a totalitarian dictatorship?

5.4 What was the influence of Italian Fascism upon right-wing politics elsewhere in Europe?

5.5 Did Mussolini wish to create a new Roman Empire?

5.6 A comparative study: Italy's entry into the First and Second World Wars

5.7 How did Italy's entry into the Second World War affect Mussolini's rule?

Framework of Events

1922	October: Mussolini appointed Prime Minister by King.
1923	Acerbo electoral law. Italian invasion of Corfu
1924	Murder of the socialist deputy, Matteotti
1925	Inauguration of 'battle for grain'
1926	Government decrees given the power of laws. Creation of special tribunal for political crimes. Rocco Law on Fascist syndicates is passed
1929	Conclusion of Lateran Accords between Italian state and Catholic Church
1934	First meetings between Hitler and Mussolini in Venice
1935	Invasion of Abyssinia (Ethiopia)
1936	Establishment of Rome–Berlin 'Axis'
1938	Introduction of anti-Semitic legislation in Italy. Mussolini deflects European conflict by his intercession in the Munich Conference
1939	Italian invasion of Albania. Conclusion of 'Pact of Steel' with Germany
1940	Italian declaration of war on France and Britain
1943	Allies invade Sicily and southern Italy Mussolini forced to resign by Fascist Grand Council.

Overview

WHEN Mussolini became prime minister, in October 1922, he had to tackle the same problems that had confronted the united Italian state throughout its existence. In terms of domestic policy, it might be argued that Mussolini was more successful than his predecessors in one respect. By direct and ruthless political methods, he put an end to the divisions and in-fighting that had marked Italian politics throughout the previous century. His great talent, perhaps his only talent, was the acquisition and advertisement of power. Most limiting factors – such as parliament, other political parties and the monarchy itself – were effectively eliminated as real forces in Italian politics. Unfortunately, it is not clear that the Fascist regime made effective use of the power that it seized. Flashy and dramatic policies were put forward for economic modernisation and for the peaceful regulation of class relations, but these appear to have made only limited progress by the end of the 1930s. At that point, of course, what gains had been made were swept away in the disastrous wreckage of Fascist foreign policy.

Before and after the establishment of Fascist government, consistent themes can be found in Italian foreign policy. Seeking to guarantee security within Europe, but also to extend the prestige of the young Italian state, Italian diplomats pursued three conflicting courses between the 1880s and the 1930s.

● The anti-Austrian theme had its origins in the *Risorgimento*, and in the subsequent demands of nationalists for further territorial gains at Austria's expense.

● The contradictory anti-French theme was also based upon territorial claims, to Nice, Savoy and Corsica, but also upon colonial rivalry in North Africa.

● The Italian desire for colonial expansion provided the third theme, which greatly complicated its relationships with the western democracies, both before and after the First World War.

1. Which of the factors in the mind map was most important in helping Mussolini create a Fascist dictatorship? Give reasons for your answer.

2. Identify three factors in the mind map which were important in helping Mussolini maintain himself in power between 1924 and 1943? Give reasons for your answer.

The difficulties that Italian diplomats experienced in choosing between these courses of action were illustrated by the abandonment of the Triple Alliance and the decision in 1915 to enter the First World War on the side of Britain and France. They can be seen again in the 1930s as Mussolini sought expansion at the same time as protecting himself against the consequences of Nazi expansion. The weak response of his British and French allies to German aggression, their apparent betrayal of Italy over Abyssinia, and the growing impression that Hitler would emerge as the dominant force in Europe, encouraged Italy once more to attach itself to what appeared to be the stronger side. In all important respects this turned out to be a terrible and fateful miscalculation, and the war that followed destroyed the Italian Fascist state. In the event, it was the fall of Italian Fascism in 1943, rather than its establishment in the 1920s, that proved to be a turning point in Italian history.

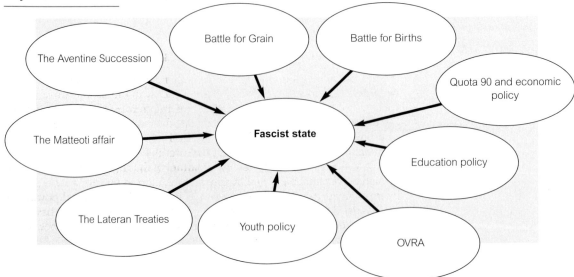

The Aventine Succession

Battle for Grain

Battle for Births

Quota 90 and economic policy

The Matteoti affair

Fascist state

Education policy

The Lateran Treaties

Youth policy

OVRA

5.1 Did the Fascist regime achieve a political revolution in Italy?

Georges Sorel (1847–1922)
Abandoning an engineering career in the 1890s, Sorel began to formulate socialist theories based upon the writings of Karl Marx and Pierre-Joseph Proudhon. The most important of these concerned the promotion of the class struggle through violence, through trade union activism, and in particular through the tactic of the general strike. Such ideas were referred to as 'anarcho-syndicalism' from the French *syndicat*, meaning a trade union.

Lockouts: The practice whereby employers might lock troublesome workers out of their place of employment, depriving them of wages, and thus forcing them to accept conditions offered by the employers.

Chamber of Fasces and Corporations: A pseudo-parliamentary system consisting of Fascist representatives drawn from administrative and industrial bodies.

Corporativism: System of government propounded by Benito Mussolini in which trade and professional organisations, or corporations, are the basis of society and political activity.

The years 1923–25 formed a period of ambiguous policy statements designed to attract the widest possible support, and of negative assaults upon existing institutions. Only slowly did the outline of a Fascist 'new order' emerge. In theory, this 'new order' owed much to the ideas of syndicalism put forward in the late 19th century by the French political thinker, Georges Sorel. In Italian hands, however, the theories of Sorel were changed significantly. From being a means towards the revolutionary overthrow of capitalism, the 'corporative' system in Italy posed as a solution to the problems of class warfare. It also served as a bridge between the factions of workers and employers in the interests of the fatherland.

What was corporativism?

The suppression of existing socialist and Catholic trade unions paved the way for the so-called Rocco Law of April 1926. This law, while outlawing both workers' strikes and employers' **lockouts**, gave legal recognition to the Fascist syndicates. Although these syndicates consisted exclusively either of workers or employers, the law provided for corporations, or 'central liaison organs', to mediate between the two. The actual implementation of this new order was extremely slow. Only in March 1930 was a National Council of Corporations created as an advisory body on the development of the system, and not until 1934 were the corporations actually set up. By 1936 there were 22 of them representing all the major branches of industrial, agricultural, artistic and professional life in Italy. Mussolini claimed to see in these corporations the logical successors to the parliament, which now had no reason to exist, he claimed, with the death of the multi-party system. Indeed, in 1938–39, the parliamentary system was abolished in name as well as in practice, and replaced by a **Chamber of Fasces and Corporations**.

In theory, therefore, the government of Italy moved towards a decentralised state in which the varying interests of workers and employers were directly represented through their corporations. In reality, in the words of the contemporary historian G. Salvemini, **corporativism** was 'an elaborate piece of imposing humbug'. For all their activity in an advisory capacity, the corporations had no role in the formulation of economic policy, which remained firmly in the government's hands. In each corporation, furthermore, the representatives of employers and workers were joined by officials of the Ministry of Corporations, whose task was to ensure that the government's view prevailed. The theory of decentralisation barely masked the reality of rigid Fascist control.

The distribution of power in the Fascist state

If corporativism did not dominate the Italian state under Fascist rule, then what did? As we have seen, much Fascist energy in the early years of power was poured into the task of disarming existing sources of influence such as the other political parties and parliament, the trade unions or the Church. The powers of the monarchy, already limited, were further restricted by measures that gave Mussolini the power to make laws by decree (January 1926), and deprived King Victor Emmanuel of the right to select the Prime Minister (December 1928). On a local level, elected mayors were replaced by nominated Fascist officials known as *podestà*. Even the local powers of the Fascist *Ras* found themselves subjected to central authority. They were unable to resist largely because their intense rivalry with each other made them so easy to isolate.

Italo Balbo (1896–1940)
A leading Fascist from the early days of the movement, and an organiser with Mussolini of the 'March on Rome' (1922). Minister for Aviation and Governor of Libya (1933–40).

Dino Grandi (1895–1988)
Joined the Fascist Party in 1922. Foreign Minister (1929–32). Italian ambassador to London (1932–39) in which capacity he was effective in disarming British opposition to Italian foreign policy. As a member of the Fascist Grand Council, he engineered the dismissal of Mussolini in 1943.

Count Galaezzo Ciano (1903–1944)
He took part in the March on Rome in October 1922, and rose to a high position within the Fascist Party (PNF). In 1930, he married Mussolini's eldest daughter, Edda. He acted as Minister for the Press and Propaganda (1934) and Foreign Minister (1936). He tried to negotiate peace with the Allies from 1942, and was a member of the Fascist Grand Council that deposed Mussolini in July 1943. He was executed for treason against Mussolini.

Elementary schools: Where children are taught for the first six or eight years of their education.

Apart from the corporations, the major new constitutional feature of the 1920s was the Fascist Grand Council. This was a body of 56 'hierarchs' (*gerarchi*), later reduced to 30, whose function as an organ of state came to include determining the succession both to the throne and to the office of Prime Minister. Even so, the powers defined for it by the laws of 1928–29 make it clear that the Grand Council, too, played only a secondary role. Its membership, times of meetings, even the agenda that it should discuss, all remained the firm prerogative of the *Duce*. In short, the end-product of the Fascist revolution was the personal dictatorship of Benito Mussolini. Two factors help to explain his success in this respect in the 1920s and 1930s. One is the comparative mediocrity of other leading Fascists. 'Most of them,' wrote Denis Mack Smith, 'were unintelligent, grasping, jealous and incompetent, and jockeyed for place by telling tales against their rivals.' Of the men closest to the *Duce* some, like Roberto Farinacci and Italo Balbo, were glorified street fighters, lacking Mussolini's political flair. Some, like Dino Grandi, were too submissive to provide firm opposition. Others, like the future Foreign Minister Galaezzo Ciano, had tied their own fate too closely to that of their leader to risk toppling him. Italian Fascism produced no Goering, no Himmler, and certainly no Röhm.

Mussolini's image and leadership

The second factor in Mussolini's favour was his own enormous talent for self-advertisement. He exploited his journalistic talents to the full, not only convincing many Italians that 'Mussolini is always right', but creating an image, far from the truth, of a man who possessed all the talents. The controlled press portrayed him as an excellent violinist, fine horseman, daring pilot, bold war hero, and as an intellectual who had mastered all the major philosophies of the day and had found time to memorise whole sections of Dante's poems. This mastery of publicity – which made him a genius at the art of seizing power – goes far to explain the disappointing record of the Fascist government. Historian Denis Mack Smith has summarised Mussolini's failings as an administrator admirably. 'Mussolini's own mental processes never ceased to be governed by slogans and eight-column headlines. He preferred to argue and speechify rather than to penetrate behind words to reality and so never properly dissected a problem. Fascism, which affected to despise speeches and talk, was itself essentially rhetoric and blather.'

Relations between State and Church

One influential element in Italian life could not be subdued or suppressed by threats and violence. Relations between Fascism and the Catholic Church remained complex throughout the 1920s. While Mussolini and other Fascist leaders never lost their fierce anti-clericalism, and both groups remained divided over the question of the education and indoctrination of youth, in other respects they shared common ground. Ever the realist, Mussolini never seriously imagined that he could govern Italy successfully with Catholic opposition. The Papacy, for all its reservations, still saw Fascism as the only alternative to the godless doctrines of socialism.

Despite an interlude of tension in 1927, when the State dissolved the Catholic boy-scout movement, Church and State extended olive branches to each other. Gentile's education act (February 1923) restored the compulsory religious education that the liberal regime had abolished in **elementary schools**. The following year, the Pope did Fascism a service by withdrawing his support from the Catholic Popular Party, an electoral rival. Always too progressive for the tastes of Pope Pius XI, the Popular

The Lateran Accords have the desired effect: schoolchildren greeting priests with the Fascist salute.

Party could not survive the blow, and Mussolini was left free of major parliamentary rivals.

These signs of mutual respect reached fruition with the signature of a batch of agreements known as the Lateran Accords (February 1929). For the Church, the Accords settled most of the outstanding conflicts between the Papacy and the Italian State. By creating the tiny state within Rome, known as the Vatican City, the State restored some of the Papacy's temporal authority. Furthermore, it confirmed Catholicism as 'the only state religion', extended compulsory religious education to secondary schools and outlawed divorce. Lastly, the Papacy received financial compensation, amounting to some 1,750 million lire, for its losses since the Italian seizure of Rome in 1870. Mussolini's gains from the Accords were less tangible, but were perhaps greater. By linking his administration with the immense moral influence of the Church, he entered upon a period of unprecedented national popularity. The Lateran Accords thus represented the greatest political success of his career and the most lasting impact of Fascist government on modern Italy.

It should not be imagined that the agreements of 1929 represented a surrender by either party. Mussolini immediately reminded parliament that the Italian state 'is Catholic … but it is above all Fascist'. In 1931 a further crisis illustrated the lines beyond which neither side would step. In that year, Mussolini declared the disbanding of the youth and student groups affiliated to Catholic Action, an educational and moral organisation highly prized by Pius XI. In the face of a papal counter-attack, Mussolini replaced the dissolution order with lesser limitations on the groups' activities. The incident illustrated the limitations upon Fascist **absolutism** in Italy, the value of silent Catholic support to the government and, thereby, the shrewdness of the understanding reached in 1929.

Absolutism: A political system in which one ruler or leader has complete power and authority over the country.

1. What was corporativism supposed to achieve in Italy, and to what extent did it do so?

2. What possible restraints were there in the Fascist State on the personal authority of Mussolini, and why were they not more effective?

3. What was achieved through the Lateran Accords of 1929 (a) for the Catholic Church and (b) for the Fascist State?

5.2 What was the impact of Fascism upon Italian culture, society and the economy?

Education and the media

The control of education was considered essential by the Fascist regime. In the classroom, the 'fascistisation' of youth involved the strict control of textbooks and of curriculum, and the removal of teachers critical of Fascist principles. The primary purpose of the school was now to teach the young such Fascist virtues as manliness, patriotism and obedience. 'A child who asks "Why?",' declared a textbook approved for eight-year-olds, 'is like a bayonet made of milk. "You must obey because you must," said Mussolini, when explaining the reasons for obedience.'

Glorification of the *Duce* was, of course, another important educational element. Outside the school, Italy set a pattern for other authoritarian regimes by the law (April 1926) which introduced a system of compulsory youth organisation to coax the male child into the required Fascist path. From four to eight the boy would belong to the 'Sons of the She-Wolf' (*Figli della Lupa*), from eight to 14 to the *Balilla*, and to the age of 18 to the 'Vanguard' (*Avanguardisti*). From 1937, the best graduates of this system might join the 'Young Fascists' (*Giovani Fascisti*) until the age of 21. Whatever the political success of the system, the Fascist years marked no great advance in conventional educational areas. Illiteracy, which stood at 48.5% in 1901, had been reduced by the liberals to 30% by 1921, but still stood above 20% in 1931.

In common with the contemporary Soviet government, Fascist Italy demanded in theory that all aspects of the cultural life of the society should support and sustain the regime. For the first time in western Europe, a government attempted to turn the communications machinery of a modern state to a co-ordinated political purpose. The press was steadily subjected to the party line by the suppression of political papers such as *Avanti!* and consistent pressure upon other editors and owners.

Fascism and sport

Sport, too, was highly prized by the regime, both as a breeder of Fascist virtues and as a source of nationalist propaganda. On a popular level, the *Dopolavoro* ('for the sake of labour') organisation was formed in May 1925. It hoped to provide for 'the healthy and profitable occupation of the workers' leisure hours', by means such as cheap holidays, libraries, lectures and theatrical entertainment. On a more elite level, several major sports were reorganised and centralised, and their international successes exploited by the state. In soccer, the 1934 World Cup competition was held in, and won by, Italy. It retained the trophy in 1938, to the great satisfaction of the Fascist regime. As boxing was naturally regarded by Mussolini as 'an essentially Fascist method of self-expression', the triumph of Primo Carnera (1933) in the World Heavyweight Championship was hailed as a further proof of Fascist virility.

The limits of cultural control

Like its ambiguous relationship with the Church, Fascism's failure to dominate Italian cultural life illustrates the limits of its absolutism. Although the movement had a considerable appeal in intellectual circles in its early days, this was partly dissipated by its later authoritarianism. The conductor, Arturo Toscanini, a Fascist candidate in 1919, left Italy for America in the 1920s. He was followed by the historian Gaetano Salvemini in 1925 and the physicist Enrico Fermi in 1938. Italy's greatest intellectual figure, the philosopher and historian Benedetto Croce, was an opponent of the regime from 1925, when he organised an anti-Fascist manifesto. Yet he not only remained in the country throughout Mussolini's years in power, but continued to produce liberal historical works, and to publish his liberal review *La Critica*. Although usually cited as an example of Fascist weakness, this might possibly be ascribed to Fascist tolerance of an influential rival, putting Croce in the same bracket as the Pope. Certainly, he would not have survived either in Nazi Germany or in Stalin's USSR.

1. By what means did the Fascist State seek to control educational and cultural activities in the Italy?

2. How justifiable is the claim that Mussolini was able to achieve a cultural revolution in Italy?

A greater failure was the inability to found any true 'Fascist culture'. Although Nobel Prizes for literature went to Grazia Deledda (1926) and to Luigi Pirandello (1936), neither was truly a Fascist. Despite the much publicised foundation of the Royal Academy of Italy (October 1929), the literature and art encouraged by the regime remained conformist, old-fashioned and lifeless. Only in engineering and music did names of international repute, such as Pier Luigi Nervi and Ottorino Respighi, emerge during the two decades of Fascist Italy.

To what extent did the Italian economy benefit from the years of Fascist government?

The abandonment of liberal economics and the return to protectionism
Italian Fascism inherited a depressing range of economic problems, including a sizeable budget deficit and a total of 500,000 unemployed. Its most consistent success in tackling these was achieved in 1922–25 when, largely for reasons of political expediency, the Ministry of Finance was in the hands of the liberal economist, Alberto De Stefani. His measures included the abolition of price-fixing and of rent controls, and the reduction of government expenditure wherever possible. His achievements included a budget that was in surplus for the first time since 1918, and a reduction in the total of unemployed to only 122,000.

Mussolini's motives for departing from this policy, and for replacing De Stefani with the financier and industrialist Giuseppe Volpi, have been the subject of debate. To Marxist commentators – of whom the contemporary French journalist D. Guerin was an extreme example – the reversion to protectionism was proof that Mussolini was doing the bidding of Italian capitalism. Heavy import duties were imposed, for example, upon grain, sugar and milk. Denis Mack Smith, however, is adamant that 'Mussolini

Mussolini delivers a speech, inaugurating work on the draining of the Pontine Marshes.

What characteristic features of Mussolini's style of government are evident in this photograph?

was no mere instrument of business and agrarian interests'. He does concede that 'his ignorance of economics and human nature left him an easy target for sharks who wanted protective duties or who extracted money from the state for quite impossible schemes of industrialisation'. An explanation consistent with other areas of Fascist policy is that Mussolini was influenced by considerations of political prestige. Certainly, the revaluation of the Italian currency the lire (August 1926) at 90 to the pound, gave it an artificial impression of strength. The immediate result of this swing to protection was that the Italian economy ran into difficulties long before the **Wall Street Crash**. The low exchange rate of the lire deterred tourist traffic and damaged trade in luxury commodities.

Wall Street Crash: Collapse of the American stock market which took place in October 1929. Nearly 13 million shares changed hands on the New York Stock Exchange on 24 October. Shock waves from the 'Crash' were felt all around the world. Many people lost a lot of money.

Autarky (or *autarchy*): Economic policy aiming at national self-sufficiency in terms of raw materials and other essential economic resources.

Pontine Marshes: the most famous area of the 'battle for land' reclamation scheme, which provided hundreds of thousands of acres of new farmland.

The battles for land, grain and births

By 1930 the government, tempted by the prospects of domestic prestige and foreign military adventures, had adopted the principle of *autarky*, that is of economic self-sufficiency. The policy bred some impressive successes, such as the five-fold increase in electricity production between 1917 and 1942, and the spectacular rise in motor production by 1941, when an estimated 34,000 cars were completed. In typically flashy Fascist fashion, however, the policy was constructed around three great national 'struggles'.

1. The 'battle for grain', officially started in 1925, was superficially successful. Production figures that had been steady at 40 million 'quintals' since 1870 rose to 60 million in 1930 and to 80 million by 1939. Some agricultural experts have pointed out that the official fixation with grain damaged other forms of agricultural output, and kept the relative cost of Italian grain production high.

2. The 'battle for land' was also marked by notable successes. Most famous of the land reclamation schemes was the draining of the **Pontine Marshes** near Rome to provide hundreds of thousands of acres of new farmland. Much of it, unfortunately, was lost again in 1943–45 due to the ravages and neglect of war. It is also well worth noting that Fascist attentions to southern Italy resulted in a more effective control of Mafia activities than was achieved before or since. In the same vein of public works, which combined public utility with political propaganda, was the construction of motorways (*autostrada*) between Italy's main urban centres, and the electrification of some 5,000 kilometres of Italy's railway system.

3. Least necessary, and least successful, of the Fascist 'struggles' was the 'battle for births'. Imagining that an increased population would provide proof of Italian virility and would support its claims for colonies, Mussolini demanded a rapid rise in the birth rate. Parents of large families were rewarded, while bachelors, with the exceptions of priests and maimed war veterans, were penalised by high taxes (1926). Abortion and contraception, of course, were outlawed. In this aim, so foolish in relation to Italy's limited resources, the *Duce* suffered bitter disappointment. Although the Italian population rose from 37.5 million (1921) to 44.4 million (1941), two different factors were primarily responsible. These were the fall in the death rate, and the restrictions placed upon immigration by the USA.

Did the Fascist regime bring about significant social and economic change?

The 'balance sheet' of the policy of *autarky* was not altogether negative. It produced some durable monuments, and served Italy well when the

Sanctions: Measures taken by countries to restrict or prohibit trade and official contact with a country that has broken international law.

League of Nations imposed **sanctions** upon it in the course of the Ethiopian War. In terms of industrial growth, however, its narrow political motives made the period 1925–40 one of the most stagnant in Italy's economic history. In those years the annual growth in productivity was only 0.8%, compared with 3.8% in 1901–25 and 3.5% in 1940–52. Cut off from the mainstream of world economics, Italy suffered recession earlier than other European powers, yet drew little benefit from the steady world recovery of the mid-1930s.

The Fascist 'revolution' in Italy failed to transform the lives of the ordinary Italians as many of its early supporters had hoped. The 'battle for land', although a potent political symbol, fell far short of any substantial change in the pattern of land ownership in Italy. In 1930, the peasant smallholder made up 87.3% of the farming population, yet held only 13.2% of the farmland. The richest 0.5% of the landed population, on the other hand, still farmed 41.9% of the available land. No significant change occurred in these proportions in the next decade. Smallholders and small-scale businessmen alike found survival increasingly difficult, with an annual average of 7,000 small farms passing to the exchequer as a result of their owners' failure to pay land tax.

Naturally, the Fascist period was for most Italians one of stagnant or declining living standards. The task of penetrating and interpreting Fascist statistics is a complex one, and researchers have differed in their conclusions. They have not disputed improvement or decline, but merely about the rate of decline. The historian Federico Chabod claims that the Italian farm labourer lost half, and in some cases more, of the real value of his wages. C. Vannutelli claims a drop in the average 'per capita' income of the Italians from 3,079 lire (1929) to 1,829 (1934). The figures have to be set against a falling cost of living and a subsequent rise of the 'per capita' income to return to the 1929 level by 1937.

Against this, one should also note the range of social benefits that the workers' syndicates secured, most of them late in the Fascist period. Sick pay was first introduced in 1928, followed ten years later by a 'package' comprising end-of-year bonuses, paid holidays and redundancy pay. Although it is possible that the lot of the worker in Fascist Italy may have been less severe than it has been painted, there is much to show that the years 1923–40 marked little improvement in the worker's life.

- The right to strike was abolished.

- The government's 'Charter of Labour' (1927) failed to guarantee a minimum wage.

- Unemployment rose from 110,000 (1926) to over a million (1933), before levelling off at around 700,000.

1. What problems did the Fascist government identify in the Italian economy, and how did it seek to solve them?

2. What aspects of Fascist economic policy, if any, may be judged to have been successful?

5.3 Was Mussolini's Italy a totalitarian dictatorship?
A CASE STUDY IN HISTORICAL INTERPRETATION

- Was Fascist Italy the personal dictatorship of Mussolini?
- How repressive was his dictatorship?
- How successful were his social and economic policies?

Framework of Events

1925	Mussolini declared his dictatorship
	Dopolavoro (OND) created
	Battle for Grain began
1926	Balilla Youth Movement created
	Ministry of Corporations established
	Special tribunal for political crimes created
	Created the secret police (OVRA)
1927	Labour Charter
	Quota 90 introduced
1928	New Electoral Law introduced
1929	Lateran Treaties with Vatican
1933	IRI created
1937	Ministry of Popular Culture created
1938	Anti-Semitic laws introduced
1943	Mussolini dismissed by the King
1943–5	Social Republic of Salo

The inter-war period in Europe (1918–39) saw the emergence of several totalitarian dictatorships of which the most notable were Hitler's Germany and Stalin's USSR. In their study, *Totalitarian Dictatorship and Autocracy* (1956), US political scientists K. Friedrich and Z. Brezinski do not mention Italy. In *The Origins of Totalitarianism* (1958), Hannah Arendt declares that 'Mussolini's fascism, up to 1938, was not totalitarian but just an ordinary nationalist dictatorship, developed logically from multi-party democracy.' The Australian historian R. J. B. Bosworth claims that Mussolini was 'the least of dictators, a hollow tyrant.' Yet the first time that the term 'totalitarian' was used in the inter-war period was in reference to Mussolini's regime. It was first used by socialists in their comparison of Fascism to previous governments. Mussolini often talked of the Fascist revolution, of creating a completely new type of state and society. But just how far was Fascist Italy a totalitarian state?

Was Fascist Italy the personal dictatorship of Mussolini?

'Totalitarian', in the Italian sense, seemed to mean the absolute rule of one man: Mussolini. In *Europe 1870–1991* (2004), T. Morris and D. Murphy declare that 'the end product of the Fascist revolution was the personalised dictatorship of Mussolini'. On the surface, this certainly seemed to be true. By 1929, Mussolini was not only Prime Minister, but also minister of eight out of thirteen departments. Mussolini was also *Il Duce* of the PNF, and he presided over the Fascist Grand Council and the **National Council of Corporations**.

In an interview, Mussolini declared that 'a leader can have no equals, no friends and give his confidence to no one.' He certainly gave the outward appearance of a dictator. In reality, however, although he was heavily built, he was below average height at 5′ 6″. He tried to disguise his shortness by standing very straight with his head leant back and his jaw jutting out. At official functions he preferred to stand next to the King, who was much shorter. He liked to wear military uniforms and had a love of fast cars, horse riding and flying. He tried to epitomise the idea of a virile, healthy ruler, but from 1925 his health deteriorated and, suffering from stomach ulcers, he was forced to follow a strict diet. Late in 1920, he went grey and subsequently shaved his head. Despite the fact that he insisted upon having at least nine hours sleep every night and refused to be disturbed for any reason, he was a hard and methodical administrator. The image of Mussolini as an all-knowing, dynamic leader was enhanced by his effective use of propaganda.

The cult of *Il Duce* became a central feature of the regime. Italians were extolled to '*Obedere, Credere, Combatere*' ('Believe! Obey! Fight!'). On 12 December 1931, the PNF Secretary, Achille Starace, introduced the ritual of *Saluto al Duce* ('Salute to the Leader') at the start of all PNF meetings. Mussolini's apparent invincibility was enhanced by his survival of three assassination attempts in 1926. Denis Mack Smith in *Mussolini, Artist in Propaganda* (1959) claims that because of this, Mussolini actually ended up believing his own publicity.

National Council of Corporations: contained corporations representing aspects of economic life. Each corporation contained representatives of business and labour. The aim was to find a 'third way' between dominance of business and dominance of labour. It was the equivalent of an economic parliament.

Achille Starace (1889–1945)
He came from a middle class family in southern Italy and was a war hero in the First World War. In 1927, he was Vice Secretary of the PNF, and became Secretary from December 1931 until October 1939. He supported the idea of enrolling millions of ordinary Italians into the PNF. In particular, he was in favour of using sport and demonstrations to encourage support for Fascism. On 28 April 1945, he was captured by Italian communist partisans near Milan, executed, and his body hung upside down, next to Mussolini's, in Milan's main square.

Mussolini shows off his physical prowess to a crowd.

Important posts held by Mussolini

Prime Minister: 1922–43
Minister of Foreign Affairs: 1924–9; 1932–6
Minister of the Interior: 1924 and 1926–43
Minister for the Colonies: 1924
Minister of War: 1924–9
Minister for the Navy: 1926–9
Minister for the Air Force: 1925–9; 1933–43
Minister for Public Works: 1929
Minister for Corporations: 1926–9; 1932–6
Commandant General of the Militia

Commandant General of the Armed Forces
First Marshal of the Empire
Chair of:
    Supreme Commission for Defence
    Council of State
    Court of Accounts
    Army Council
    Supreme Council of Statistics
    Permanent Committee on Cereal Production
    Committee on Civilian Mobilisation
    National Council of Corporations
    Fascist Grand Council

Totalitarian Dictatorship

In 1956, C. Friedrich and Z. Brezinski outlined what they saw as the key characteristics of a totalitarian dictatorship:
- A charismatic leader with an elaborate ideology
- A one-party state
- A terror police force
- Complete state control of education, culture and propaganda
- Complete state control of the economy
- Complete state control of the armed forces.

In *Italian Fascism* (1989), Alexander De Grand claims that Mussolini's dictatorship went through two distinct phases: one of consolidation (1925–35) and one of decline (1935–43). Renzo de Felice entitled the two volumes of Mussolini's biography, which cover 1936 to 1943, *The Totalitarian State* (1981), implying that there was a change in policy from that date. In its next phase, the regime is seen as having been more dependent on the 'myth' of Mussolini.

Mussolini secured control through a 'divide and rule' tactic. In 1923, he established the Fascist Grand Council, which shared decision-making with the **cabinet**. Mussolini was the link between these two bodies. Also, Mussolini had no serious rivals. However, he is seen to have had limited control over the King, Catholic Church and to some extent the Fascist Party.

Cabinet: the senior committee of government.

Relations with the King

Even though Mussolini was dictator, a constitutional monarchy still remained in existence and the King had the right to dismiss Mussolini at any time. On a number of critical occasions – most notably during the Matteotti affair of 1924 – he had the chance to do so, but declined. The King was never willing to confront the 'Fascist revolution in government' before the Second World War because the alternative may well have been chaos, and the rise to power of socialism. Although his relationship with the King was never very friendly, Mussolini always showed due respect. The King even remarked that Mussolini was one of his most respected Prime Ministers.

However, relations became strained in March 1938, when Mussolini announced that he had made himself First Marshal of the Italian Empire, a post without precedent and which had a quasi-royal dimension. The King made it clear to Mussolini that he disliked this development, but he acceded to Mussolini's decision to replace him as Commander-in-Chief of the Italian armed forces in times of war. Finally, however, it was the King who on 25 July 1943 dismissed Mussolini as Prime Minister.

Relations with the Vatican and Italian Catholic Church

One of Mussolini's greatest domestic achievements was the settlement between the Italian State and the Vatican, which Mussolini himself claimed was his most memorable triumph.

The creation of an Italian State between 1859 and 1870 had resulted in a major crisis in Church–State relations. Up to 1870 the Pope had had two roles: spiritual head of all Catholics throughout the world, and ruler of an Italian State, the **Papal States**. Pope Pius IX (1846–78) refused to recognise the Italian State and instructed Catholics not to participate in Italian politics. However, an improvement in Church–State relations occurred in 1919 when Pope Benedict XV (1914–22) allowed the creation of the Catholic Political Party, (PPI).

It took Mussolini – who as a young man was anti-clerical – to bring about a settlement. Negotiations between the government and the Vatican began in August 1926. Francesco Pacelli, whose brother became Pope Pius XII in 1939, represented the Vatican; Domenico Barone represented the government. By 11 February two agreements were reached.

The first agreement was the Lateran Treaty, between the Italian State and the Pope, which granted the Pope a small independent state within Rome, known as the Vatican City State. In return, the Pope recognised the Kingdom of Italy, and Victor Emmanuel III as King. This re-established the Pope's independence, which he had lost in 1870. The Pope also received 750 million lira in cash and one billion lira in government bonds as compensation for property taken from the Vatican. The second agreement between the Italian State and the Catholic Church was the **Concordat**, which determined the role of the Catholic Church within the Fascist state. The Concordat dealt mainly with education and marriage: the government extended Catholic religious instruction in schools from primary to secondary level; textbooks had to be approved by the Church; and religious marriages were recognised by the government. Mussolini also agreed to the independence of the youth section of Catholic Action.

Papal States: the last part of the Papal States, the Patrimony of St Peter, with Rome as it capital, became part of the Italian state in 1870. From that moment on the Pope lost his political independence. Technically, he became an Italian citizen. It started a period known as the 'Babylonian captivity of the Papacy'.

Concordat: an agreement between an independent state and the Vatican about Church–State relations.

Mussolini and Church Dignitaries posing at the Lateran Palace, Rome, after the signing of the Concordat (1929).

This agreement with the Church was important to Mussolini for a number of reasons. First, it increased the regime's popularity with Catholics. Secondly, it was an important factor in the overwhelming support given to Mussolini in the March 1929 referendum. Thirdly, it brought the Catholic Church within the Fascist regime in Italy. Finally, it increased Mussolini's international standing as a statesman, in Catholic countries in particular.

This does not mean that relations between Church and State were always cordial after 1929. In fact, a major rift occurred in 1931 when Mussolini attempted to disband the youth section of Catholic Action. On 9 July 1931, the government declared the merger of the youth section of Catholic Action with the Fascist youth movement, the *Ballila*. The Pope issued an **encyclical** *Non abbiamo bisogno* ('We have no need') against the declaration. Through an intermediary, Father Tacchi-Venturi, the Pope threatened to excommunicate Mussolini if he did not revoke this declaration. Thus on 2 September, the government announced that the youth section of Catholic Action would remain independent but would not compete in sporting activities, limiting itself instead to educational and religious matters.

Encyclical: a pronouncement by the Pope.

Another rift occurred in 1938 over the government's introduction of anti-Semitic laws. Mussolini's increasingly close relationship with Adolf Hitler was responsible for this complete change in Fascist policy. On 3 August 1938, the Ministry of Education was prohibited from allowing foreign Jews (refugees) into schools. On 1 September Mussolini issued a decree forbidding foreign Jews to settle in Italy, Libya or the Dodeconese Islands and, the following day, all Jews were dismissed from teaching posts. Finally, on 6 October, the Fascist Grand Council announced that Italians would not be allowed to marry Jews and that Jews were forbidden to join the PNF or the armed forces. In Milan, **Cardinal** Shuster condemned these laws in a pastoral letter to all Catholics in his archdiocese. The Pope, who was a strong critic of Nazi Germany, also condemned Mussolini's policies against the Jews.

Cardinal: a senior cleric of the Catholic Church who has the right to elect the Pope.

Relations between the Vatican and Mussolini only improved from March 1939 when Pius XI died and was replaced by Pius XII (1939–58). Pius XII had been Papal Nuncio to Nazi Germany and had signed a concordat with Hitler.

Relations with the Fascist Party (PNF)

The Fascist movement, and from November 1921 the Fascist Party (PNF), had been a coalition of different interests. The moderate Fascists were willing to tolerate Mussolini's adoption of the constitutional path to power; extreme Fascists simply yearned for a Fascist revolution. From 1925 Mussolini brought the PNF under effective central control. Under the secretariat of Roberto Farinacci (1925/6) dissent within the PNF was silenced. Farinacci was an ex-railway worker and socialist with a violent and erratic personality. Mussolini replaced him in 1926 with Augusto Turati, who ensured that regional power bases within the PNF were liquidated. On 9 December 1928, the Law on the Powers of the Grand Council made the Fascist Grand Council State-controlled under Mussolini's leadership. Turati was succeeded by Giovanni Giurati from October to December 1931, who was later replaced by Achill Starace who remained Secretary of the PNF until October 1939. Starace made sure that the PNF did not provide an alternative power base for any rival to Mussolini. Starace widened PNF membership to include ordinary workers and peasants, which diluted the control of Fascist regional bosses. By the outbreak of the Second World War, the PNF attracted careerists and job seekers rather than revolutionaries.

How repressive was Mussolini's dictatorship?

Having announced a dictatorship in his speech to Parliament on 3 January 1925, Mussolini spent the next two years creating one. On 21 November 1925 he began by reintroducing capital punishment for treason. On 26 November, a law was issued governing all associations within Italy: all associations had to register with the police, as did their members; any breach of the law would lead to the closing of the association. This law applied to all political parties, and by November 1926, all deputies of the opposition had been expelled from parliament.

On 24 December 1925, a law decreed that any public servant could be dismissed for disloyalty to the government. On the same day, the post of Prime Minister was also changed to Head of Government. This meant that Mussolini reported to the King and not Parliament. On 31 January 1926, Mussolini acquired the power to rule by decree. In other words, he could make his own laws. A decree law passed on 31 December made newspaper owners liable for their editorial. It also created a journalists' association from which all anti-Fascists were excluded. All of these laws were reinforced by fascist violence. In *The Rise of the Fascist State* (1974), Italian historian Alberto Aquarone describes the 'intense campaign of intimidation, violence, confiscation, and suspension [that] was waged against the opposition press, which was finally reduced to silence. The squads also stepped up their attacks … [and the] police also intervened with ever-increasing frequency, issuing warning and ordering suspensions. The Italian press was completely muzzled.'

On 31 January 1926, a law was passed that denied Italian citizenship to anyone who committed an act that disturbed public order. Some of the first victims were Gaetano Salvemmi, an historian, and Giuseppe Donati, a Catholic journalist, who had both criticised the Fascists over the Matteotti affair. They subsequently lost all of their property. On 6 April 1926, a law extended central control over local government, and a subsequent law of 7 July 1926 abolished all local elections.

Thus by the end of 1926, Mussolini had removed the two main areas of opposition to his rule: parliament and a free press. From 3 April 1926, all cinemas were ordered to show official government newsreels, which were merely fascist propaganda. By 1930, approximately 66 per cent of all newspapers were controlled by the Fascists, and those newspapers that were not under their control received daily instructions on what to write on political matters.

In December 1926, the 'Law for the Defence of the State' was passed, which created a secret police and a special tribunal for political crimes. Arturo Bochinni was given the task of organising this secret political police force, OVRA. Bochinni served as chief of OVRA from 1926 to 1940 and was regarded as the third most powerful man in Italy after Mussolini and the King. Historians Denis Mack Smith and R. J. B. Bosworth claim that the name OVRA was chosen by Mussolini because it sounded sinister. However, in *Fascist Italy* (1968), Alan Cassels states that it stood for *Opera Volontaria per la Repressione Anti-fascista* ('Organisation for the Repression of Anti-Fascism'). In its operation, OVRA was far less oppressive than other security police, such as the Gestapo and SS in Nazi Germany, or OGPU and NKVD in Stalin's USSR; it was also rather small, employing just 375 staff. An important punishment used by OVRA was *confino* where the victim was forced to live either on the Lipari Islands, north of Sicily; on the isles of Tremiti off the Adriatic coast; or on the mainland at Amalfi and Cava dei Tirreni. However, although the penal settlement on the Lipari islands was hard, elsewhere internees were lodged in cottages of their own choice.

The special tribunal and OVRA were used simultaneously. In all 13,547 cases that were dealt with by 1943, 27,742 years of imprisonment were imposed. Between 1927 and 1943, the Fascist regime imposed 42 death sentences for political crimes, of which 31 were carried out, 22 of these during the Second World War. Ethnic groups that suffered particular persecution were Slovenes in the Trieste area, and after 1938, Jews.

It would seem on the surface that Mussolini's dictatorship, although repressive, was popular. On 24 March 1929, a referendum on the regime was held. More than 8.5 million people voted 'yes' in support of the regime; only 135,000 people voted 'no', with 8092 spoilt ballot papers.

The importance of propaganda and leisure

Mussolini once remarked that governing the Italian people wasn't hard: 'To govern them you need two things, policemen and bands playing in the streets.' Like other dictators, Mussolini used propaganda and sport to encourage support for the regime. State newsreels extolling the virtues of Fascism were seen in all cinemas. The press was effectively controlled. Government policies, such as the draining of the Pontine Marshes near Rome, received massive publicity. The archeological sites of ancient Rome were restored, causing much damage to Renaissance buildings.

Mussolini was also aware of the importance of sport. In 1934, the Italian football team won the World Cup when it was held in Rome. In Paris, in 1938, they repeated their performance. Also, the Italian Primo Carnera won the World Heavyweight Boxing title in 1933. These sporting victories were exploited by the regime as examples of the superiority of Fascism.

An important factor in Mussolini's ability to maintain control was *Dopolavoro* ('for the sake of labour'), a fascist after-work organisation created in May 1925. It was the principal means by which Mussolini regulated the leisure hours of the adult, working population. It covered virtually everything that could be classed as 'mass culture': from sporting events to movies, from listening to the radio to going to the theatre. Membership, which rose from 300,000 in 1926 to 3.5 million in 1939, was voluntary. This comprised 40 per cent of the industrial workforce and 25 per cent of the peasantry. By the outbreak of war in 1940, the OND (Opera Nationzale Dopolavoro) ran 1227 theatres, 771 cinemas, 2130 orchestras, 6427 libraries and 11,500 sporting groups. It was the most popular Fascist organisation.

How successful were Mussolini's social and economic policies?

There is much debate as to whether Mussolini had clear aims in his economic policy. He certainly inherited a number of serious economic problems, most notably a sizeable budget deficit and an unemployment level of 500,000. Therefore, his aim when he came to power in 1922 was to create economic stability.

Initially, economic policy was placed under the control of Alberto Di Stefani, a liberal economist. His policies included abolishing price fixing and rent controls, and reducing government spending where possible. By 1925, he had successfully reduced unemployment to 122,000, and the government was in surplus. In July 1925, Di Stefani was replaced by Giuseppe Volpi, who settled Italy's war debts with the USA and Britain, and obtained a US loan of 100 million dollars.

Mussolini controlled the Italian economy through government intervention. However, historian Alexander De Grand argues in *Italian Fascism*

Mussolini sows the first seeds in the new province of Littoria, which was reclaimed from the Pontine Marshes in the 'battle for land'.

Protectionism: the placing of duties or quotas on imports to protect domestic industries against foreign competition.

Confindustria (handwritten)

(1989) that although the regime 'altered the role of the state in Italian economic life … these changes were largely forced on the regime by events rather than implemented by any preconceived plan'. The first government economic policy was the introduction of **protectionism**. In August 1926, the government also imposed an exchange rate of 90 lira to the pound, which made the Italian currency seem more powerful. However, this made Italian exports more expensive and increased Italy's economic difficulties long before the Wall Street Crash caused a world economic depression at the end of 1929.

The most innovative aspect of economic policy was the so-called creation of the Corporate State. Mussolini had always claimed that he was against class conflict between workers and employers; the Corporate State was meant to act as a model for economic and industrial harmony by uniting Italian Society. This began in 1926 when Guiseppe Bottai created a Ministry of Corporations, which controlled various branches of economic activity including industry, agriculture and commerce. In 1930, a National Council of Corporations drew together employer and worker organisations, which by 1934 had been refined and developed into mixed

Economic Indices for Italy: 1929–38

1938 = 100

Year	Industrial Production	Cost of living
1929	90	102
1930	85	99
1931	77	90
1932	77	87
1933	82	82
1934	80	78
1935	86	85
1936	86	85
1937	100	93
1938	100	100

corporations of workers and employers. Finally, in 1939, a Chamber of Fasces and Corporations was established to which corporations sent representatives. It meant to settle industrial disputes equitably between employer and worker, but in reality it favoured the employer. This favouritism reinforced the dominance of business over labour. Free trade unions were abolished and replaced by fascist equivalents, which meant that all disputes were to be settled under the guidance of the Fascist State. The statutory eight-hour day was replaced by a nine-hour day. In the following year, the Charter of Labour was introduced, which referred all labour disputes to a labour court appointed by the Government. Finally, it made work 'a social duty'; voluntary withdrawal of labour (a strike) became a punishable offence.

An important Fascist economic institution was the *Instituto per la Reconstruzione Industriale* (Institution for the Reconstruction of Industry or IRI), set up in 1933. It was a state-financed body for helping weak companies to survive the economic depression. However, it favoured large businesses, taking many into public ownership. By 1939, 70 per cent of iron production, 45 per cent of steel production, 80 per cent of naval construction, and almost all shipping and parts of the electrical and telephone industries were taken over by the IRI.

Mussolini always couched economic initiatives in military language. In June 1925, he launched the 'battle for grain', aimed at reducing dependence on imports by increasing domestic production. This was quite an effective policy, reducing imports by 75 per cent by 1940. In 1927, the 'battle for the lira' created **Quota 90**. Finally, the 'battle for births' aimed to increase the Italian population by reducing emigration and increasing the birth rate. The population increased from 37.5 million in 1921 to 44.4 million in 1941.

Mussolini's ultimate aim for economic policy was autarky. This was accelerated after 1936 when the League of Nations placed economic sanctions on Italy for invading Ethiopia. The economy grew at a yearly average of only 0.8 per cent between 1925 and 1940, compared to 3.8 per cent between 1900 and 1925, and 3.5 per cent between 1940 and 1952. This was partly due to the economic depression after 1929. The index of **real wages** fell 11 per cent between 1925 and 1938. In the countryside too, no significant changes occurred. In 1930, the peasantry comprised 87 per cent of the population but owned only 13 per cent of the land. Overall, the average per-capita income of Italians fell from 3079 lira in 1929 to 1829 lira by 1934. Unemployment also rose to one million by 1933.

Unfortunately, Italy's economic growth under Fascism was one of the slowest in the twentieth century. Compared to its competitors (Britain, Germany, France and the USSR), Italian economic development was limited. In 1940, the Italian economy was still in a weak state and unable to meet the demands of war effectively, an important factor in the Italian defeat.

Italian historian Cesare Vannutelli sums up Fascist economic policy in *The Living Standard of Italian Workers, 1929–1939* (1958) when he states:

> 'Italy suffered more than other countries from the world crisis of 1930–2 because its economy had already been weakened by the revaluation of the currency (Quota 90 in 1927). Unlike other countries, Italy could not benefit from economic recovery in the 1930s because of the policy of autarky. Consequently, Italy's economic development lagged behind that of other countries.'

Quota 90: the decision to change the international value of the lira from 150 to the pound to 90.46 to the pound sterling, which Mussolini believed showed Italy's economic stength. In reality, it made Italian exports more expensive and imports cheaper.

Real wages: the money a person receives when inflation (rising prices) has been removed. It refers to the 'purchasing powers' of wages.

The impact of Fascism on youth

The fascist regime placed great emphasis on the indoctrination of the Italian youth. Every attempt was made to incorporate youth into the party and state structure. On 3 April 1926, the *Opera Nazionale Ballila* ('National Youth Organisation') was created for young people aged six to 18 years. The aim was to organise activities outside of school hours. In 1930, the *Fascio Giovanile del Littori* ('Fascist Juvenile Group') was set up for 18 to 21 year-olds. At university level, a separate organisation, the *Gruppo Universitari Fascisti*, aimed to sustain fascist propaganda. However, its membership was small and unenthusiastic. Nevertheless, these organisations were central to Fascism's attempt to reach the mass of the Italian population. In October 1937, all youth movements were unified as the *Gioventu Italiano del Littorio* ('Italian Fascist Youth' or GIL) under the control of the PNF. By 1939 the two youth movements had eight million members.

Impact on education

The regime also altered the education system to ensure its influence. In every classroom a portrait of the King had to be accompanied by one of Mussolini. University professors were forced to take an oath of loyalty to the regime. School textbooks were altered to emphasise the 'cult of *Il Duce*'. In a compulsory textbook for eight year-olds it stated that 'the eyes of Il Duce are on every one of you …. What is the duty of a child? Obedience!'

Impact on women

Radical social change was not only limited to youth. Fascism also had a major impact on women. In their Programme of 1919, the Fascists promised women the vote and social equality. However, this did not occur when they took power. With the 'battle for births' the regime constantly emphasised the role of women as home-makers, whose main function in life was to bring up children. 'Mother and Child Day' was introduced and became officially recognised from 1933. To train future mothers, the *Piccole Italiane* (for girls aged nine to 14) and the *Giovani Italiane* (for girls aged 15 to 17) were set up. From the mid-1920s, a popular slogan of the PNF was *le donne e casa* ('women into the home'). This coincided with the creation of the *Opera Nazionale de Maternita e Infanzia* ('national organisation for child rearing' or OMNI), which supervised the welfare of mothers and children. From 1929, working mothers received maternity leave and welfare payments. Taxes were even placed on bachelors to encourage marriage. These developments received powerful support from the Catholic Church.

Giovanni Gentile, the Minister of Education from October 1922, restricted the numbers of female teachers in secondary schools. Preference was also given to men in government employment. In 1938 a law was passed limiting the number of women in the workforce to just 10 per cent. Women had their own organisation within the Fascist Party, the *Fasci di Femminili*, or women's auxiliaries. It published its own periodicals, *Giornale dell Donna* ('Mothers' Journal') from 1924, and *Vita Femminile* ('Female Life') from 1926. The aim of the organisation was to support fascist programmes on the family. By 1935, it had only 400,000 members compared to two million men in the PNF.

Republic of Salo

Following his rescue by German paratroops in September 1943, Mussolini created the Social Republic of Salo in German-occupied north Italy. From

September 1943 until his death in April 1945, Mussolini presided over this German puppet-state. Real power resided in the hands of General Wolff of the German army. Mussolini declared that the Republic was against the traitors who had ousted him in July 1943, including Fascists such as Grandi, the monarchy, the armed forces and the civil service. In reality, there was little difference between the policies that he followed before and after September 1943. His main support came from pro-Germans, anti-semites and the remnants of the PNF.

The Salo Republic had no capital. Foreign affairs were dealt with from Salo, defence from Cremona, Corporations from Verona, education from Padua, and justice from Brescia. It had neither an army nor any diplomatic recognition beyond Nazi Germany and its allies. The nearest it got to a constitution was the programme produced by the Verona Congress of the reformed PNF in November 1943. It was republican, pro-Catholic and anti-Semitic. In economic matters it promised a 'third way' between capitalism and socialism. Under a law of February 1944, all large businesses were placed under state control. In *Mussolini* (1981) Denis Mack Smith argues that in the Salo Republic, Mussolini 'reasserted the socialist beliefs of his youth', claiming that he had never deserted the Fascist programme of 1919, which contained a strong socialist core.

By late 1944 even Mussolini began to backtrack on his anti-Semitic policies, claiming that they were opportunist and had been a mistake. By early 1945 he was blaming the Germans for his predicament. He regarded Hitler as a fanatic and a 'thorough-going authoritarian'. He regarded himself as authoritarian 'only on the surface'. On 28 April, he suffered the ultimate humiliation of being captured and executed by Italian communist partisans and subsequently being displayed hanging upside-down in the main square of Milan where Fascism had been born in March 1919.

Source-based questions: Was Mussolini's Italy a totalitarian dictatorship?

1. Read the following extract and then answer the question.

Fascist rule
'Since 1922 Italy has been living under a dictatorship. For 12 years Italy has enjoyed a government established by force and maintained by force and by the exclusion of all alternative opinions. The word democracy must be left out of the question altogether. The Italian regime is a dictatorship. Fascism is Mussolini: that is the judgement of most Italians. It has all his strength and weakness and while he is great he is mortal. Fascism will perish with Mussolini, leaving as a heritage the problem of establishing a government suitable for the average Italian. This can hardly be accomplished peacefully.'

(Adapted from Herman Finer's *Mussolini's Italy*, Victor Gollanz Press, 1935, page 11.)

Using the extract, and information from this section, how far do you agree that Fascist rule was the personal rule of Mussolini?

2. To what extent did Fascism control the lives of all Italians from 1925 to 1945?

5.4 What impact did Italian Fascism have on other right-wing politics in Europe?

The conquering political idea of the inter-war years?

Considering the steady collapse of liberal democratic forms of government throughout Europe in the 1920s and 1930s, it would be tempting to see Mussolini as the founder of the conquering political idea of the era. By the end of the 1930s, authoritarian governments had been established in Germany, Spain, Portugal, Hungary, Austria, Romania, Yugoslavia and Poland. Even in France democracy was under severe strain. One should not exaggerate, however, the international influence of the Italian Fascist form of government which Mussolini himself had declared earlier in his career was 'not for export'.

Many apparent similarities between Fascism and these other movements result not from conscious imitation by the latter, but from common features in the movements' origins. Hungary, like Italy, received a strong nationalist impulse from the supposed injustices of the peace treaties, and the short-lived socialist regime of Bééla Kun (1919) which left an even stronger anti-communist feeling than the one which had helped Mussolini to power. The threatening closeness of the Soviet Union also stimulated anti-Marxist passions in Hungary, Poland, Finland and Romania alike.

The extent of Italian influence on the European right

When Italian Fascism did directly influence its 'sister' movements, it was in the one area where Mussolini showed true mastery – in the tactics of the seizure and consolidation of power. There can be little doubt of the direct influence upon Hitler of the Fascist use of salutes, uniforms and rallies as means of fascinating the public, and of the use of organised violence to terrorise one's enemies. In Germany, however, these tactics remained means to other ends, whereas in Italy they too often appeared as ends in themselves. Much later, Adolf Hitler remained fond of referring to Mussolini as 'his only friend', and of claiming that it was the Italian's example that had given him the initial courage to pursue his own political ambitions. In Hitler's consolidation of power many elements, such as the suppression of the press and of the trade unions, had close parallels in Italy. Throughout Europe, especially where Fascist movements struggled to achieve power, the rituals and trappings of Italian Fascism were imitated in Oswald Mosley's British Union of Fascists, among the French *Cagoulards*, and in the Romanian Iron Guards.

Direct imitations of Italian ideology or methods of government are, however, harder to detect. Corporativism appeared in the right-wing programmes of Antonio Salazar in Portugal and of Engelbert Dollfuss in Austria, while the Italian 'Charter of Labour' (1927) found echoes in Spanish 'Falangist' policy and in Portugal. Neither had any parallel in the Nazi movement. The French *Cagoulards* and the Austrian *Heimwehr* were rare in having direct contact with the Italian government. In many cases, it is easier to pick out direct contrasts with Italian Fascism. The Catholicism that Mussolini tolerated because he could not defeat it was a central factor in the **authoritarianism** of Dollfuss in Austria and of the *Falange Espanol*. The Orthodox Church played an equally strong role in the thoughts of Codreanu, creator of the Romanian Iron Guard movement. Where Italian Fascism had made, in effect, a prisoner of the monarchy, the Spanish dictator Primo de Rivera was mainly motivated by an unswerving loyalty to the Crown. Totalitarianism, to which Mussolini aspired, but which only Hitler perfected, was not seriously sought by Primo de Rivera, by Dollfuss, or by Pilsudski in Poland. Their opponents continued to operate in public,

Authoritarianism: Political system favouring or enforcing obedience to the authority of the state, to the detriment of personal liberty.

Falange Espanol (**'Spanish Phalanx'**): A nationalist and elitist group founded (October 1933) by José Antonio Primo de Rivera. It was influenced by the tactics of the Nazis.

albeit often under difficult conditions. In short, it is as easy to overestimate the international influence of Italian Fascism, as it is to exaggerate the united nature of right-wing politics in inter-war Europe. As Elizabeth Wiskemann remarked, in *Fascism in Italy* (1969), 'Italian Fascism was not the conquering creed of the 20th century', but merely in some superficial respects 'led a political fashion for two decades'.

The influence of Nazism upon Italian Fascism

By the late 1930s, there was increasing evidence that Fascism itself was coming strongly under the influence of more dynamic forces. Several of the means by which Mussolini sought to revive his regime appeared to be reflections of German practices, although he strongly denied it. The Ministry of Popular Culture (*Minculpop*), set up in June 1937, played much the same role as Josef Goebbels' Propaganda Ministry. Above all, the range of anti-semitic legislation which successively forbade foreign Jews to enter Italy (September 1938), and banned Italian Jews from public, academic and party posts (November 1938), seemed absurd in a country with so little previous history of anti-semitism. It could only be seen as an imitation by Mussolini of his more forceful partner. Such a trivial matter as the introduction of the 'goosestep' into the Italian army, under the new title of the 'Roman step' (*Passo Romano*), convinced many of the extent to which 'Fascism in Italy lost its character and became a poor imitation of German National Socialism' (Elizabeth Wiskemann).

1. In what respects, if any, did Italian Fascism truly influence other right-wing movements in Europe in the 1920s and the 1930s?

2. How convincing is the argument that Fascism in the 1920s and 1930s should be seen as a consistent and coherent European movement?

5.5 Did Mussolini wish to create a new Roman Empire?

■ What were his foreign policy aims?

■ Was the Ethiopian War the major turning point in foreign policy?

■ Was he Hitler's puppet?

Framework of Events

1923	Corfu Incident
1924	Italy annexed Fiume
1925	Italy signed the Locarno Treaties
1926	Italy occupied Albania
1934	Nazis fail in their attempt to unite Germany and Austria
1935	Stresa Front against German conscription and rearmament
	Italy invaded Ethiopia
1936	Outbreak of Spanish Civil War. Italy sent aid to Franco
	Rome-Berlin Axis
1937	Anti-Comintern Pact with Germany and Japan
1938	*Anschluss* of Germany and Austria
	Munich Crisis
1939	Italy annexed Albania
	Pact of Steel
	Germany invaded Poland, Second World War begins
1940	Italy declared war on Britain and France
1941/2	Italy defeated in Ethiopia and Libya
1943	Sicily and mainland Italy invaded by Allies
	Mussolini sacked by King
1943–5	Social Republic of Salo in north Italy

Mussolini's foreign policy is a matter of considerable debate among historians. When he came to power as Prime Minister in October 1922, some of his biographers, such as Denis Mack Smith, claim that he did not have a clear aim in his foreign affairs. Rather, Mussolini is portrayed as an opportunist. However, important questions require discussion. Were Mussolini's foreign policy aims merely a continuation of the policies pursued by his liberal predecessors? Or, was there a distinct Fascist foreign policy? German historian, Fritz Fischer, highlighted how domestic issues influenced the agenda for foreign affairs. How far were Mussolini's foreign ventures dictated by domestic concerns? Was he the peacemaker of Europe, or an aggressor who destabilised inter-war Europe, making the Second World War more likely? Was Mussolini's foreign policy racist? Finally, was there a turning point in Mussolini's foreign policy at which it became more aggressive and expansionist? These questions are central not only to any study of Mussolini, but also for studies of Italian and European history. The Second World War plunged the European continent into six years of carnage. During the war, Italy lost its entire overseas empire, was invaded, and suffered a two-year civil war. Mussolini clearly played a pivotal role in these events.

1. Which of the points in the mind map do you regard as Mussolini's greatest success in foreign and imperial affairs? Give reasons for your answer.

2. Place all the points in the mind map in two columns – 'Successes for Mussolini' and 'Failures for Mussolini'. Do you think any of the points had elements of both success and failure? If so, which one(s)?

3. Was Mussolini successful in foreign and imperial policy before 1940, and a failure thereafter?

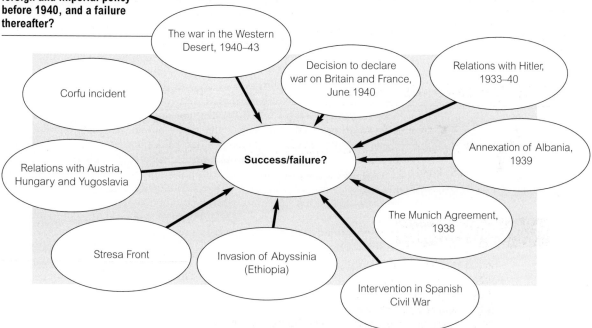

What were Mussolini's foreign policy aims?

In *Italian Fascism* (1989), historian Alexander De Grand claims that 'when the fascist government took power in October 1922, little thought had been given to foreign policy'. Yet one of the reasons why Mussolini split from the PSI in 1914 was because of foreign affairs. Mussolini's decision to support Italy's entry into the First World War on the side of the Allies was the major turning point in his political career.

Canadian historian, Alan Cassels, supports the view that foreign affairs were, in fact, central to Mussolini's thinking. In *Fascist Italy* (1969), he claims that 'the drive for a totalitarian society was nothing more or less than an endeavour to escape dependence on foreign powers. In the last resort Italy's international status was the criterion by which Mussolini's regime would stand or fall.' Mussolini's main aim was to obtain international advantage for Italy, which would reflect on his position as *Il Duce*. Australian historian, R. J. B. Bosworth expands on this in *Mussolini* (2002) when he claims:

> 'from the beginning of his career Mussolini had mostly directed his aspiration to be a 'Great Man' by advertising his expertise in international affairs. This is reflected by Mussolini's personal -involvement. For most of his regime he had direct control over the ministry of Foreign Affairs. In the 1930s he worked closely with his son-in-law, Count Galaezzo Ciano. Mussolini also had control over the ministries associated with the armed forces. In the 1930s he also took on another political title, 'First Marshal of the Empire.'

In *Hitler's Italian Allies* (2000), McGregor Knox believes that 'like Hitler, Mussolini believed he was a man of destiny whose task in life was to make Italy 'respected and feared' in international affairs.'

The merger between the Fascists (PNF) and Nationalists in 1923 led to important developments in Mussolini's foreign policy, which involved the acquisition of many of the Nationalist Party's aims. Part of the merger agreement involved Mussolini adopting a more aggressive foreign policy, supported by strong armed forces.

Indeed, Denis Mack Smith's study of Mussolini's foreign policy suggests that he wanted to recreate a modern Roman Empire by expanding Italy's colonial territories in East Africa. In 1922, Italy controlled Libya in North Africa and owned Italian Somaliland and Eritrea in East Africa. Ethiopia (historically known as Abyssinia), which lay next to these Italian colonies, was an obvious target for Mussolini, particularly since there had been a long-standing feud concerning the exact border between Ethiopia and these territories. Mussolini believed that Ethiopia was within Italy's sphere of influence and hoped to reverse the humiliation that the nation had faced during the military defeat by the Ethiopians at the battle of Adowa in 1896. On a broader scale Mussolini hoped to acquire Anglo-Egyptian Sudan, thus uniting all his African territories into one geographical unit.

Italy's colonial ambitions were not limited to Africa. Mussolini also had aims to extend Italian power and influence around the Adriatic and the Balkans. His aim of making the Adriatic Sea an 'Italian lake' led him to apply diplomatic pressure on Yugoslavia to give him Fiume, which Italy felt they deserved as payment for their **mutilated victory**. It also involved acquiring Albania and undermining the Kingdom of Yugoslavia, which controlled the Dalmatian coast, by supporting Croat separatists who wished to break from Yugoslavia. This led, indirectly, to the assassination of King Peter of Yugoslavia and the French President by a Croat terrorist in Marseilles in 1934.

Mussolini also strove for Italian domination of the Mediterranean, which brought Italy into conflict with Britain. One of Mussolini's greatest achievements was the expansion and modernisation of the Italian Navy. This enabled Italy to acquire Malta (a British colony and naval base) and destabilise British influence in Egypt. The invasions of Greece and Egypt in late 1940 were also part of this strategy. Rather naively, Mussolini tried to persuade Hitler to abandon his ambitions towards the USSR and support Italy in its attempt to control the Mediterranean.

Aside from Mussolini's aim of expanding the Italian empire, domestic considerations were also important in his conduct of foreign policy. Improving Italy's international standing was seen as effective propaganda for increasing support for the regime. In *Mussolini's Roman Empire* (1976), Denis Mack Smith claims that Mussolini was glad to sign treaties because

'Mutilated victory': the idea that Italy won the First World War but lost the peace. Italy did not receive all the territory promised to her by the Treaty of London in April 1915, which brought Italy into the war.

The extent of the Italian Fascist Empire in 1940.

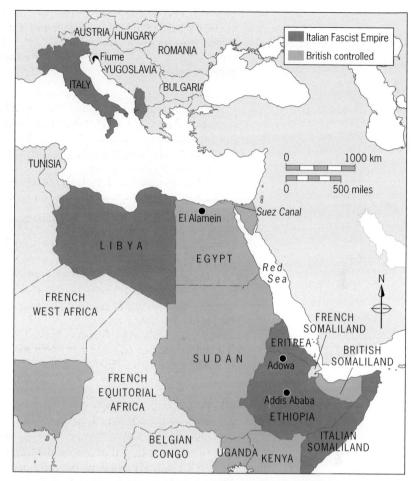

treaties meant news. From 1935 to 1936 the regime's popularity significantly increased because of the successful invasion of Ethiopia. Another domestic issue was the onset of the world economic depression in 1929. Italy, more than most other European states, was adversely affected. The development of a more aggressive foreign policy in the 1930s can be explained in part as diverting domestic attention away from economic concerns.

Mussolini's foreign policy aims: change or continuity?

Historians have long debated the degree to which foreign policy actually changed under Mussolini's control. Did he develop a unique Fascist foreign policy? Or, did Mussolini simply follow the same policy that had been set up by his liberal predecessors? In terms of his policy of colonial expansion, in *Mussolini* (2002) R. J. B. Bosworth is emphatic that:

'Even at its most aggressive, Fascist Italy behaved as though it were a nineteenth-century power, replicating the grab for Africa indulged by the Greater Powers at that time.'

He suggests that rather than break from his liberal past, Mussolini's aim to expand Italian influence simply continued the themes that had shaped Italian foreign policy before his rise to power. However, other historians have identified distinct Fascist characteristics in Mussolini's views on foreign affairs. In *Mussolini's Early Diplomacy* (1970), Alan Cassels claims that the Corfu Incident of August 1923 constituted a change from earlier policy. He believes that this incident – caused by the murder of an Italian general by Albanian terrorists on the Greek island of Corfu, which led the Italian navy to bombard Corfu – 'disclosed the nature of Fascism's foreign policy. It constituted a dress rehearsal for Mussolini's quarrel with the League of Nations over Ethiopia in 1935'.

A truly Fascist foreign policy can be seen to have developed in 1926 with the resignation of non-Fascist Salvatore Contarini, the Secretary General of the Foreign Ministry, after Dino Grandi, a leading Fascist, became involved with foreign affairs. The complete 'fascistization' of foreign affairs came from 1936, when Count Galaezzo Ciano, Mussolini's son-in-law, was appointed as Foreign Minister. From this time, foreign policy involved providing a tremendous amount of support for international Fascist-style movements. In *Mussolini's Roman Empire* (1976), Denis Mack Smith outlines how Mussolini allowed right-wing paramilitary groups, such as the Nazis, to train in Italy; gave support to the Heimwehr, a right-wing paramilitary movement in Austria; provided approximately 60,000 pounds per year to Oswald Mosley and the British Union of Fascists; and offered money to the 'Blueshirts', an Irish Fascist group. Mussolini also planned to destabilise the Kingdom of Yugoslavia by forming an alliance with Hungary and providing financial support for separatist movements in Macedonia and Croatia.

The biggest display of this style of foreign policy was Mussolini's support for Franco and the Nationalists in the Spanish Civil War (1936–9), which Germany also supported. Mussolini supplied aircraft to transport Franco's troops from Spanish Morocco to mainland Spain in 1936. He also dispatched a large number of men and war material to support Franco over the duration of the war. By 1937, Italy had 35,000 men fighting in Spain in the *corpo truppo voluntaria* ('volunteer corps' or CTV). The degree of Italian intervention in the Spanish Civil War far exceeded that of Nazi Germany and the USSR (who supported the Republican side). By the end of the war, 3819 Italians had been killed and approximately 12,000 wounded. In monetary terms it had cost between 12 and 14 billion lira, equivalent to two years' military expenditure. This included the provision of 250,000 rifles, 2000 artillery guns and 750 aircraft for Franco's Nationalist cause, equal to a third of Italy's military might.

Was the Ethiopian War the major turning point in foreign policy?

Historians usually divide Mussolini's foreign policy into two distinct phases. In the 1920s Mussolini is portrayed as having followed a relatively passive foreign policy. While he still wanted to gain respect from the Great Powers, he was much more cautious in his approach. This is evident in his support of the Franco-Belgian occupation of the Ruhr, an industrial area of Germany, which occurred because Germany was late in paying reparations. Similarly, in 1925, Italy was also one of the major signatories of the Locarno Treaties, which confirmed Germany's post-1919 borders. The treaties were regarded as a major breakthrough in ensuring peace and stability in Europe. In 1928, Mussolini, along with most European countries, signed the Kellogg-Briand Pact, which renounced war as a diplomatic weapon. To a certain extent these policies were successful in increasing Mussolini's respectability, particularly from Britain. The British Foreign Secretary, Austen Chamberlain, believed that it was only a matter of time before Mussolini would become a moderate. This view was echoed by the British ambassador of Rome, Robert Graham. However, Denis Mack

Smith believes that Mussolini, rather than being passive and cautious, used foreign policy as a propaganda exercise to further the cause of Italian Fascism abroad. This is especially apparent in Mussolini's suggestion of moving the secretariat of the League of Nations from Geneva to Rome.

During this period of passive foreign policy, Mussolini was also successful in his acquisition of the Adriatic port of Fiume, which many Nationalists had been demanding since the First World War. At the Paris Peace Conference, the Dalmatian coast, which the Allies had promised to Italy, was instead awarded to the newly created Kingdom of Yugoslavia. Italy only received the port in 1924, after it was seized and occupied by Gabriele D'Annunzio from 1919 to 1920, and following a period of diplomatic pressure by Italy.

Italian influence in the Adriatic also increased from November 1926 when King Zog of Albania signed a treaty, which gave Italy economic control of Albania. From 1927, Italian army officers trained the Albanian army. Italy later became responsible for Albania's administration. Eventually, in 1939 Albania was formally **annexed**, and King Zog deposed. Mussolini had also succeeded in controlling the Straits of Otranto, which formed the entrance to the Adriatic Sea from the Mediterranean.

In colonial affairs Mussolini achieved some success when in 1925 Britain **ceded** Jubaland to Italian Somaliland. Later, in March 1935, Italy also joined Britain and France to create the Stresa Front: an international attempt to defend the Treaty of Versailles against Germany's announcement to reintroduce military conscription.

During the 1930s Mussolini's foreign policy is considered to have become much more aggressive. The most obvious example of this was the invasion of Ethiopia. The reasons as to why this change occurred have caused much debate among historians. Biographer Renzo de Felice argues that the change occurred when Mussolini appointed leading Fascist, Dino Grandi, as Head of Foreign Affairs in 1929. Historian G. Carocci believes that changes in policy did not occur until later, over the period 1932 to 1935. In *Mussolini as Empire Builder* (1977), Esmonde Roberston offers a different explanation, placing emphasis on the death in December 1931 of Mussolini's younger brother, Arnaldo, who Roberston regards as having been a major restraining influence on Mussolini's naturally aggressive temperament. However, Roberston also cites an important meeting between Mussolini and Pope Pius XI on 11 February 1932 at which the Pope warned Mussolini about the growth in the influence of Protestants, Jews and Communists. Mussolini had just experienced a serious rift with the Vatican over the youth section of Catholic Action and the *Balilla*. In this way Mussolini's decision to extend Italy, and with it Catholic influence, can be seen as a way to appease the Pope. Several historians, including Roberston and Mack Smith, identify the economic depression in Italy as an important motivating factor in Mussolini's change in approach to foreign affairs. Success abroad would certainly have diverted attention away from growing economic problems.

Finally, as R.J.B. Bosworth points out, Mussolini can be seen to have fulfilled the traditional Italian policy of imperialism by reversing the defeat of Adowa of 1896 and conquering part of East Africa, which was within Italy's sphere of influence. Italy invaded Ethiopia on 3 October 1935 following a border incident at Wal Wal the previous year between Ethiopia and Italian Somaliland. Mussolini employed brutal methods including poison gas and the massacre of approximately 400,000 Ethiopians, and easily defeated the outdated Ethiopian Army.

The Ethiopian War can be seen as a turning point in Mussolini's overseas policy. Although the conquest gained him increasing prestige and popularity in Italy, it was condemned by the League of Nations who

Annex: to take over territory from another country.

Ceded: to give territory to another country.

imposed economic sanctions on Italy. However, these sanctions were rather weak because they excluded key goods such as petroleum products. Furthermore, Britain did not close the Suez Canal to Italian shipping, which would have cut Italy off from Ethiopia, and the USA (which was not a member of the League of Nations) continued to trade with Italy. Despite this, however, Italy still made the decision to leave the League of Nations in 1937. In international terms this meant that Italy, along with Japan and Germany, was seen as a state that wished to upset international peace and stability.

The outbreak of war did not end attempts by British and French diplomats to woo Mussolini. In the secret **Hoare-Laval Plan** of 1935, two senior British and French politicians attempted to appease Mussolini by offering Italy a partition of Ethiopia. However, once this 'pact' became public knowledge in Britain and France it caused outrage, and was subsequently dropped by both governments. Ultimately, the Ethiopian conquest signified the growing gulf between Italy and the western democracies and further aligned Italy with Germany.

A new direction in foreign affairs was signalled by the appointment of Mussolini's son-in-law Count Galeazzo Ciano as Minister of Foreign Affairs. Ciano paved the way for a closer relationship between Mussolini and Hitler, which was to have tragic consequences for Mussolini and Fascist Italy.

Some historians still regard Mussolini as Europe's peacemaker, even after 1935. In *Roma tra Londra e Berlino* (*Rome between London and Berlin*) (1980), Italian historian Rosaria Quartararo claims that Italy remained pivotal in ensuring European peace. She states that Mussolini was central in the achievement of the Munich agreement over Czechoslovakia in

Hoare-Laval Plan (7–8 December 1935): named after British Foreign Secretary, Sir Samuel Hoare and French Foreign Minister, Pierre Laval. It planned to partition Ethiopia, leaving Ethiopian emperor Haile Selassi with some territory. The plan was rejected by the British and French governments on 18 December 1935, but not by Mussolini.

Hoare-Laval plan for the partitioning of Abyssinia (Ethiopia).

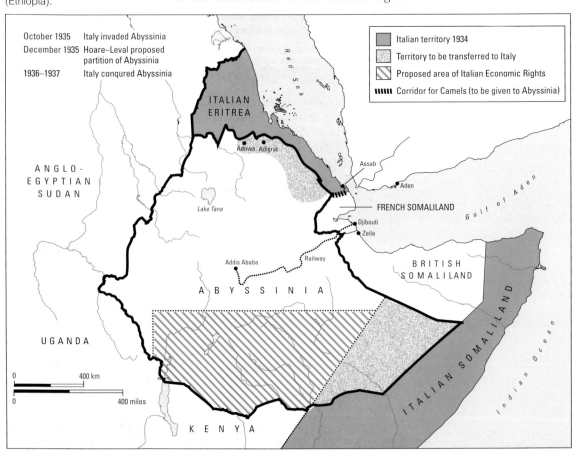

September 1938 and that the 'European war did not break out on 1 October 1938 only because Fascist Italy did not want to go to war.' Again in August/September 1939, as Hitler prepared to invade Poland, Mussolini is portrayed as trying to mediate between Germany, Britain and France. He is seen as the 'real arbiter' of the crisis. It was only on 9 June 1940, once Mussolini was convinced that Germany had defeated France and would shortly do the same to Britain, that he reluctantly committed Italy to war on Hitler's side.

Was Mussolini Hitler's puppet?

Mussolini's association with Hitler created the impression that the two right-wing dictators were united in a common ideological foreign policy. What historian F. W. Deakin called 'the Brutal Friendship' was born from Mussolini's decision to invade Ethiopia in October 1935. Up to that point, Mussolini had cooperated with powers such as Britain and France. In fact, Mussolini was exceedingly wary of Hitler's designs on Austria from 1933 to 1935 because he regarded Austria as within his own sphere of influence. In 1934, Austrian Nazis had attempted to seize power by assassinating the Austrian Prime Minister, Engelbert Dolfuss, an ally of Italy. To prevent a Nazi takeover, Mussolini moved four divisions of the Italian army to the Austro-Italian border and engaged in a propaganda campaign against them. Italian action was an important factor in preventing a German-Austrian union.

Comintern: the Communist International organisation set up in Soviet Russia in 1919 to spread the ideology of communism around the world.

However, from October 1935 Mussolini became increasingly associated with Nazi Germany. In 1936, the Rome-Berlin Axis announced their mutual support. This collaboration was expanded to include Japan with the signing of the Anti-**Comintern** Pact in 1937. In December 1937, an

Mussolini and Hitler watch a Nazi parade in 1937.

Anschluss: the forcible union of Germany with Austria.

economic agreement was concluded between Germany and Italy whereby Italy agreed to import more German manufactured goods. In return, Italy sent 30,000 agricultural labourers to work in Germany. By 1939 Italy had become increasingly dependent on Germany, for coal imports in particular.

By March 1938, when Hitler took control of Austria in the **Anschluss**, Mussolini stood back and did nothing. On 22 May 1939 Germany and Italy consolidated their relationship with the Pact of Steel which brought the two Fascist powers into alliance. Italy agreed to commit all of its armed forces if Germany became involved in a war. Also, both sides agreed to consult each other if international events threatened war. However, Mussolini regarded the pact as 'yet another piece of paper' that had little bearing on future Italian action. Thus when the Second World War began on 3 September 1939, Mussolini decided to remain neutral. Finally, in June 1940 Mussolini joined Germany in its war against Britain and France. From that moment on Mussolini was tied to Hitler's shirt-tails. When Hitler launched **Operation Barbarossa** against the USSR in June 1941, Mussolini provided an Italian army to assist Germany and its other allies (Romania, Hungary and Finland). In Yugoslavia, Greece and North Africa, Italian and German troops fought side by side. When the war turned decisively in the Allies' favour after the battles of El Alamein (November 1942) in North Africa and Stalingrad (Sept. 1942 to Feb. 1943) on the Eastern Front, Mussolini's fate seemed sealed. The Anglo-American invasion and occupation of Sicily in July 1943 brought about Mussolini's downfall on 25 July that year.

Operation Barbarossa: the surprise attack on the USSR by Germany and its Allies from 22 June 1941.

Was Mussolini's foreign policy racist?

A controversial aspect of Mussolini's foreign policy that suggests a break with the past is the racism that occurred both in Italy's colonial territories and in its policies in Europe during the Second World War.

A central aim of Mussolini's foreign policy was to link Fascist Italy with the glory of the Roman Empire. Fascist propaganda always tried to make this link: the cult of *Il Duce* mirrored the adulation once heaped on Roman Emperors; the adoption of the Roman salute as the Fascist salute was an outward symbol of this association; the adoption of the Roman 'fasces' as the Fascist symbol – the axe surrounded by a bundle of sticks was the ancient Roman symbol of justice – was representative of Mussolini's vision of Italy as ruling inferior races, both in Africa and in the Balkans.

In many ways this mirrored the colonial ambitions of Italian governments prior to the First World War. However, there was a new intensity and brutality to Mussolini's policies. In Libya, between 1928 and 1933, the Italians used excessive force to subdue the resident Arab population.

General Pietro Badoglio (1871–1956)

Mussolini's Senior General, a Marshal of Italy and briefly Mussolini's successor in 1943. He was Army Chief of Staff from April 1925 and became Governor of Libya from September 1928 to December 1933, using extreme methods to quell a local Arab uprising. Although he initially opposed the Ethiopian War, he became Italian commander in Ethiopia from November 1936, and again in 1939/40. He led the failed invasion of Greece in 1940. He resigned on December 4 1940, following accusations of incompetence from leading Fascist, Roberto Farinacci. Following Mussolini's arrest on 25 July 1943, the King appointed him as Chief of Government. He negotiated a ceasefire with the Allies behind the backs of the Germans.

General Rodolpho Graziani (1882–1955)
Major colonial general, Chief of Staff and Minister of Defence in the Social Republic of Salo, 1943–5. He pacified Libya from 1932 to 1933 and was appointed Governor of Somaliland in 1935. He led the southern front in the Ethiopian War and was an extremely brutal colonial administrator. He was in charge of the Italian North African Army in December 1940 when it was routed by the British under General Wavell. He retired from the army in 1941 and received a 19-year prison sentence after the war, but only served his sentence until 1950 when he became head of the Neo-Fascist Party, the MSI.

Ethnic cleansing: describes the murder of a population on the basis of race. An alternative term is genocide.

Under the Governorship of General Badoglio, the Italian colonial government engaged in a policy that would now be termed **ethnic cleansing**. In 1930, in a bid to end local opposition to Italian rule, the Italians drove out an Arab population of 100 000 from the interior. Displaced families were put in concentration camps on the Libyan coast. When the camps were closed in September 1933, only 50 per cent of the original inmates had survived. In fighting the local insurgent Omar al-Mukhtar, the Italians used poison gas. In September 1931, al-Mukhtar was put on trial and publicly hanged. In Ethiopia the Italians adopted similar tactics: poison gas, aerial bombardment of civilian targets, and indiscriminate massacres characterised the military campaign. General Graziani claimed: 'The Duce shall have Ethiopia with the Ethiopians or without them, just as he pleases'. Indro Montanelli, a Fascist journalist who fought in Ethiopia, proclaimed: 'We shall never be the dominators if we don't have an exact consciousness of our destined superiority. We do not mix with blacks. We cannot, we must not.' In July 1936, Mussolini appointed General Graziani as Viceroy of Ethiopia and gave him instructions to follow a policy of terror and extermination. Following a grenade attack by Ethiopian insurgents on 19 February 1937, the Italians retaliated by massacring over 3000 Ethiopians.

In Europe, Italian racism was also apparent. In Yugoslavia, Italian troops forced Orthodox Christian Serbs to convert to Catholicism. The Italians also supported the Ustace, the Croat military force that engaged in ethnic cleansing against the Serbs.

An even more problematic area of Mussolini's overseas policy was his association with the Holocaust. In 1938, the Fascist government introduced anti-Semitic laws. Italian Jews, unlike those of Eastern Europe, were integrated into mainstream society. By 1942 reports had reached Mussolini's government of the onset of '**The Final Solution**' against Jews in Poland. Although there is evidence that Italian officials were slow and obstructive in meeting German demands to hand over Jews in Tunisia, France and Yugoslavia, Mussolini eventually acceded to German demands on the issue. In June 1942, Italian troops engaged in a roundup of Jews in Croatia.

'The Final Solution': the German plan to murder the entire European population of Jews and Gypsies.

Following his dismissal by the King on 25 July, and the subsequent creation of the Republic of Salo, Mussolini's link with the Holocaust became clear. As a puppet of the German administration in north Italy, Mussolini had to accept the deportation of the Jews to the death camps in occupied Poland. By the spring of 1945, with his regime on the brink of collapse, Mussolini claimed that his racial policies had always been opportunistic and that he regretted his involvement in Hitler's anti-semitic campaign.

Was Mussolini a complete failure in foreign affairs?

Foreign policy: creating a new Roman Empire?

Ultimately, Mussolini was overthrown because of his failures in **foreign policy**. Yet, during his regime, Italy's standing among the European powers increased. In many ways Mussolini did achieve his aim of making Italy a nation to be respected and feared – foreign affairs did aid the survival of his regime at home; the invasion and occupation of Ethiopia won support in 1936 from the Catholic Church, industrialists and nationalists. Italian philosopher, Giovanni Gentile claimed: 'Mussolini today has not just founded an empire in Ethiopia. He has made something more. He has created a new Italy.' Historian Renzo de Felice describes the conquest of Ethiopia as 'Mussolini's masterpiece'.

However, the Ethiopian War did not come without a cost: nearly an entire year's annual revenue for the government. In addition, the cost of replacing lost military equipment amounted to the equivalent of the military budget for three years. When combined with the cost of the Italian involvement in the Spanish Civil War, Mussolini's foreign adventures had almost bled Italy dry by 1939. Italy was the first major European state to rearm after the First World War. As a result, much Italian military equipment was obsolete by the outbreak of the Second World War. The lack of finance to engage in a modernisation programme after the Ethiopian War helps to explain Italy's poor military performance from 1940 to 1943.

The conquest of Ethiopia did not produce the economic benefits that Mussolini had hoped for. By 1941, only 3200 Italians had emigrated to Ethiopia. In its short life (1936–41) the Ethiopian Empire never ran at a profit. In the end, Mussolini's dream of a great East African Empire was short lived. In 1941, British troops from Kenya and Sudan overran the territory with relative ease. The War also forced Mussolini into a relationship with Hitler and so, from 1936 to 1943, Mussolini's fate in foreign and imperial affairs were dependent on Hitler's success. When Hitler failed to achieve his military aims in the Second World War, Mussolini was doomed.

Source-based questions: Mussolini's Foreign Policy Aims

1. Read the following extract and answer the question.

There is no doubt that Mussolini was moved by the desire to wipe out the memory of the defeat of the Italians by the Ethiopians at the Battle of Adowa, in 1896. But mingled with this desire for vengeance was the ambition to extend Italy's overseas possessions. The mirage of a modern Roman Empire beckoned.

If he was to match the position of Britain and France in the world, he must also possess overseas territories, from which, so he argued, he could export his surplus population.

Adapted from *Mussolini: Study of Demagogue* by Sir Ivone Kirkpatrick, Odhams Press, 1964, pp,292–3

Using information from the extract, and information from this section, what were Mussolini's aims in overseas policy?

2. How far did 1935 mark a turning point in Mussolini's foreign and imperial policy

5.6 A comparative study: Italy's entry into the First and Second World Wars

Twice in the first half of the 20th century – in 1914 and in 1939–40 – Italy found itself on the fringes of an international crisis that threatened Europe with general war. In both cases it chose to intervene, with drastic consequences. From the viewpoint of a British or a French commentator, the two decisions may at first seem very different. One appears as the brave decision of a democratic government to side with other democratic regimes, and the other as a piece of cynical opportunism on the part of a Fascist dictator out to share in the spoils of an immoral war. Viewed in a broader context, however, it may appear that the logic behind the two decisions was similar and that they demonstrate the continuity that existed in Italian history between the creation of the united state and the fall of Mussolini.

Historians have largely turned away from the traditional left-wing interpretation that Italy went to war in 1914 at the suggestion of its capitalists, and particularly of armament manufacturers. The socialist writer, Guiliano Procacci (*History of the Italian People*, 1970) points out that there is little evidence for this. He adds that, as American industrialists demonstrated, it was often more profitable to remain neutral and thus to sell weapons to both sides. Most recent writers have viewed the decision as a diplomatic one, based upon considerations of security and of possible territorial gain. Martin Clark, in *Modern Italy 1871–1982* (1984), concludes that the decision was relatively sound. Austria had already breached the terms of the Triple Alliance by failing to consult its ally over its actions in the crisis of 1914. Italy was justified, therefore, in standing aloof as the crisis unravelled. Yet neutrality involved risks of its own, and it was dangerous to abandon one set of allies without cultivating another. The prospect of siding with the Entente powers seemed much more attractive by the end of 1914, for the French victory on the Marne had thwarted German hopes for a rapid victory, and perhaps their hopes of any victory at all. An Entente victory, of course, held the promise of territorial losses for Austria, and subsequent gains for Italy.

Historians C.J. Lowe and F. Marzari, in *Italian Foreign Policy 1870–1940* (1975), lay the emphasis slightly differently, stressing that Italy regarded Britain as the major factor. If Britain remained neutral, then Italian participation on the side of Germany and Austria-Hungary remained viable. If Britain fought against those states, however, its naval power in the Mediterranean made it impossible for Italy to contemplate opposition. Just as they had done in the great wars of the *Risorgimento*, Italy attempted to persuade Austria to surrender territory as the price of neutrality, rather than as the prize for military victory. Only when Austria refused did the Italian government conclude its agreement with Britain and France.

A more sinister interpretation of these events is that Italy entered the war through one of the most blatant examples of that 'secret diplomacy' which the US President Woodrow Wilson condemned so roundly in 1919. This interpretation continues to emphasise the motive of territorial gain, but makes intervention the responsibility of a narrow, élite group of Italian politicians. It claims that the Prime Minister, Sidney de Sonnino, and the Foreign Minister, Antonio Salandra, guarded their secrets so closely that parliament was not consulted, and even the army commanders remained ignorant of government policy until war was almost upon them. Where other states may have been able to blame patriotic agitation and widespread **jingoism** for their involvement in the disasters of the war, many sectors of Italian society showed a distinct lack of enthusiasm. Italian historian A. Monticone, in *Da Giolitti a Salandra* (1969), concluded that 'Salandra, when signing the Pact of London, was fully aware that he was acting against the great majority of the Italian people.' Three hundred parliamentary deputies

Jingoism: Fanatical and unreasonable belief in the superiority of your country, especially when it involves support for a war against another country.

protested, industrialists feared that their supplies of raw materials would dry up and the veteran Italian statesman Giovanni Giolitti expressed the opinion that 'the people in the government deserve to be shot'.

In the 1930s, Mussolini's government responded to the increasing instability of Europe by reversing this diplomatic process. Working at first with Italy's First World War allies, Britain and France, he later cultivated close relations with Germany, culminating in military intervention on Hitler's side in 1940. In Martin Clark's view, Mussolini was playing the same diplomatic game as his predecessors. Having gained little from friendship with the liberal democracies, either in terms of security or territory, Italy drifted towards Germany in part to wring concessions from the British and the French, and to resurrect the alliance of the early 1930s with specific gains for Italy. It might even be claimed that, with considerable prestige won at Munich as the saviour of European peace, and with the annexation of Albania in 1939, the policy had its successes. Lowe and Mazari view Mussolini's growing friendship with Hitler as a relatively responsible and sensible policy. Given the consistent hostility with which Italian policy was now viewed by London and Paris, 'Rome could not help but reflect that Germany was her only reliable friend. If the choice facing Italy was either isolation or alliance with the Reich, the alliance always carried with it the possibility – or the illusion – of exercising restraint on Germany's dynamism.'

Why, though, did Italy sign the Pact of Steel in 1939, committing itself to military support for Germany? It has been argued that, even then, Mussolini sought short-term Italian gains from the crisis, rather than an all-out war for which Italy was scarcely prepared. 'His policy in 1938–39,' Martin Clark writes, 'was essentially still that of manoeuvring for advantage among the contending powers, meanwhile hoping that a European war could be avoided.' Lowe and Marzari suggest that Mussolini certainly saw it as an 'alliance with the strong', and thus as a guarantee of Italian security, but was greatly reassured in 1939 by the assumption that it would be at least three years before any hostilities would begin. 'That such a war-free period was crucial to his policy,' Lowe and Marzari have concluded, 'cannot be doubted.'

Mussolini's biographer, Denis Mack Smith (*Mussolini*, 1981), takes a more negative view of Mussolini's actions in 1939. His account is of irresponsible and heavy-handed **war-mongering**. Mussolini, he claims, was fully aware of Hitler's plans over Poland when he signed the Pact of Steel, and simply hoped to use the destabilisation that Hitler's attack on Poland would cause to further his own ambitions in the Balkans and in the Mediterranean. Worse still, these plans were unrealistic and unclear. 'He thought once again of taking Tunisia or Algeria, and the chiefs of staff were told to have plans ready for an attack on Yugoslavia and Greece. These were hardly the actions of someone dedicated to the cause of peace, as he later claimed, nor did they have much contact with reality.' Mack Smith is severely critical of Mussolini's diplomacy, and of his political realism in the months leading up to the war. Mussolini was out of his depth at this stage. He was prone to put propaganda in the place of serious preparation, and approached the crisis with armed forces that he knew to be inadequate for a prolonged modern war. This was not the first time, however, that Italy had found itself in this position. Mussolini's misconceptions about the war that he was undertaking in 1940 were therefore not unlike those of Italy's leaders when they approached war in 1914.

When war suddenly flared up in 1939, as in 1914, the first Italian response was to stand aloof from the conflict, and to pursue a policy of non-belligerence. Yet to shirk the German alliance now, after years of Mussolini's rhetoric about territorial revision and decadent democracies, would place the Fascist regime in an impossible and embarrassing

War-mongering: Encouraging people to expect war or trying to get a war started.

position. As had happened in 1914, the crisis advanced at a faster rate than Italian policy had anticipated. Mussolini, like Sonnino and Salandra in 1914, based his decision upon events in northern France. Where the French had won a great victory in 1914, they collapsed utterly in 1940. Mussolini's final decision to go to war was motivated by the assumption that German victories in northern France in 1940 were decisive. It was the worst of many miscalculations.

Overall, the fact remains that the fateful decisions of 1915 and 1940 were made without any serious reference to ideology. Both were informed by the traditional realities of Italian foreign policy. As ever, Italy lacked the resources to initiate or to steer European diplomacy. On the other hand, it remained sufficiently attractive as an ally to be courted by the major powers, and to anticipate substantial rewards for its support. Such a policy, in the years of the *Risorgimento*, formed one of the bases for Italian unification. In 1914–18, the same policy achieved mixed results. Italy found itself on the winning side, but appeared to be cheated of the rewards that it had been promised. In 1940–45, the policy was attempted for the third time. This time, Italy's leader had seriously miscalculated the nature of the conflict in which he sought to participate, with fatal consequences for regime and leader alike.

---

1. What different interpretations have been provided by historians of Italy's decisions to go to war (a) in 1915 and (b) in 1940?

2. What arguments are there for and against the claim that in 1915 and in 1940 alike, it was broadly in Italy's best interests to go to war?

5.7 How did Italy's entry into the Second World War affect Mussolini's rule?

What was the military and economic impact of the war upon Italy?

Mussolini's decision to join the war in 1940 was a calculated gamble. He anticipated a short campaign, directed primarily against France, and resulting in cheap, but significant, territorial gains. At first, everything went according to plan, for France had surrendered within two weeks of Italy's intervention. Elsewhere – in North Africa, in the Balkans, and subsequently in Russia – the fighting continued. Italy had made absolutely no preparation for such campaigns, and for all Mussolini's warlike propaganda, its forces were ill-equipped to sustain them. The campaign that Mussolini launched against Greece (October 1940) ended in disaster as the Greeks drove Italian forces back into Albania, and the loss of five warships at the Battle of Cape Matapan (March 1941) ensured that naval supremacy in the Mediterranean would lie with the British. By the summer of the same year, nearly 400,000 Italian soldiers had surrendered to the British in North Africa. Despite German aid, Italy had lost all its African possessions by the beginning of 1943. In each of these theatres of war, the Italian campaigns had been chaotic, with adequate equipment for only 35 of the 75 divisions that the army put in the field. As he held the offices of Minister of War, Minister of the Navy and Minister of the Air Force, as well as the rank of Supreme Commander, Mussolini's personal responsibility was direct and undeniable.

economy

Just as the Italian armed forces were unable to meet the requirements of a modern, technological war, so the Italian economy lacked the means to adapt. Above all, Italy suffered in this respect from its lack of raw materials and energy resources. Hydro-electric power could not easily be increased to meet wartime demands, oil resources in Libya had not yet been detected, and steel production actually declined in the course of the war, leaving Italy largely dependent upon hand-outs from its German allies. To make matters worse, Italian industrial centres were systematically bombed by the allies from the autumn of 1942 onwards. In many combatant states, the war effort provided a stimulus to industrial production; in Italy it went some way towards wiping out the limited progress that had already been made. 'Northern Italy,' Martin Clark concludes, 'was one of the few places where aerial bombing proved effective in the Second World War. It disrupted production, it shattered morale, and it forced thousands of people to flee from the cities.' Inevitably, low levels of wartime production were accompanied by a virtual breakdown in the production of consumer goods. The recruitment of thousands of peasant soldiers also had a severe impact upon levels of food production.

What was the political response to military failure?

Under such circumstances, the pretence and propaganda of the Fascist party and its leaders quickly crumbled. Indeed, Mussolini himself delivered none of his characteristic public addresses after mid-1940. Local officials in Sicily began to ignore government directives, and Italian control of newly acquired territories in the Balkans crumbled in the face of powerful resistance movements. From 1940 onwards, the Germans actually began to govern the South Tyrol (*Alto Adige*) as part of their own territory. A major strike in Turin (March 1943) provided the first evidence that anti-Fascist political groups within Italy were beginning to exploit the economic and social chaos. Liberals, socialists, Communists and Catholics all began to produce their own anti-war propaganda, and their own versions of Italy's best escape route from this disaster.

Despite the post-war claims of such groups, however, it was not their activity that ultimately undermined the Fascist regime. Like many of the leaders who fell from power in the course of the 20th century, Mussolini was ousted because he lost the support of the élite groups that had initially supported him. Army officers, aristocrats and church leaders were deeply involved in the conspiracies that began to form in 1942–43. Mussolini's decision to sack a large proportion of his **Cabinet** in February 1943 ensured that a number of prominent Fascists also turned against him. By that time, Ciano and other prominent members of the Italian establishment had been in contact with the allies for several months, attempting to negotiate a safe and honourable withdrawal from the war. The central, co-ordinating figure was King Victor Emmanuel III himself, equally concerned to limit the harm done to his country, and to ensure the future of his dynasty.

The final crisis of the Fascist government was precipitated by military events in July 1943, when allied troops landed in Sicily, quickly occupying the island, and when allied aircraft bombed Rome for the first time. Under these conditions the Fascist Grand Council met (24 July 1943), itself a rare event, and voted to end Mussolini's personal dictatorship and to return supreme political authority to the King. The following day, Victor Emmanuel dismissed and arrested Mussolini, and appointed Marshal Badoglio in his place.

As it had risen from obscurity as a consequence of one world war, the Fascist regime now collapsed because of its failure in a second conflict. In the longer term, and like all other aspects of Italy's wartime activities, this coup failed in all respects. While Marshal Badoglio hesitantly negotiated an armistice with the allies, German forces anticipated Italian intentions, entered the country and seized strategic points including the capital itself. This ensured that the worst aspects of Italy's involvement in the Second World War were still to come. For a further year the population and **infrastructure** of the state suffered terrible damage as Italy became a major battlefield between Germany and the allies. Mussolini's political career was also resurrected briefly, in humiliating fashion, as he was snatched from captivity by German commandos and installed as the 'puppet ruler' of a Fascist republic in northern Italy (1943–45). There he finally met his death at the hands of Communist resistance fighters in the final days of the war.

Cabinet: Group of the most senior and powerful ministers in a government who meet to discuss and decide policies.

Infrastructure: The basic structure on which a country, society or organisation is built, such as the facilities, services and equipment that are needed for it to function properly.

Source-based questions: Mussolini's foreign policy, 1936–1940

SOURCE A

The German ambassador to Rome reports a conversation with Mussolini in January 1936.

Mussolini received me this afternoon. He thought that it would now be possible to achieve a fundamental improvement in German–Italian relations and to dispose of the only dispute, namely, the Austrian problem. Since we had always declared that we did not wish to infringe Austria's independence, the simplest method would be for Berlin and Vienna to settle their relations on the basis of Austrian independence, e.g. in the form of a treaty of friendship with a non-aggression pact, which would in practice bring Austria into Germany's wake. If Austria, as a formally quite independent state, were thus in practice to become a German satellite, he would have no objection.

From a report by the German ambassador to the German Foreign Office, 7 January 1936.

SOURCE B

The Italian Foreign Minister comments upon Mussolini's aims in foreign policy in 1938

It seems to me that there is not much hope of a *rapprochement* [coming together] with France. The *Duce*, in my usual interview with him, traced the lines that our future policy will have to follow. 'Objectives: Djibouti, at least to the extent of joint rule and neutralisation; Tunisia, with a more or less similar regime; Corsica, Italian and never gallicised, to be ruled directly; the frontier to be pushed back to the River Var. I am not interested in Savoy, which is neither historically nor geographically Italian. This is the general pattern of our claims. I do not specify one or five or ten years. The timing will be settled by events, but we must never lose sight of this goal.'

From the Diary of Count Ciano, Italian Foreign Minister, 8 November 1938

SOURCE C

The Italian Foreign Minister comments upon Mussolini's decision not to go to war in 1939

The *Duce* is calm. He has already decided not to intervene, and the struggle that has agitated his spirits during these last weeks has ceased. He telephones personally to Attolico [the Italian ambassador in Berlin] urging him to entreat Hitler to send him a telegram releasing him from the obligations of the alliance. He does not want to seem untrustworthy in the eyes of the German people, nor in the eyes of the Italian people, who, to tell the truth, do not show too many scruples, blinded as they are by anti-German hatred.

From the *Diary of Count Ciano*, Italian Foreign Minister, 1 September 1939

SOURCE D

The Italian Foreign Minister comments upon Mussolini's decision to go to war in 1940

Mussolini begins to talk as follows: 'Some months ago I said that the allies had lost the victory. Today I tell you that they have lost the war. We Italians are already sufficiently dishonoured. Any delay is inconceivable. We have no time to lose. Within a month I shall declare war. I shall attack France and Britain from the air and from the sea.' Today, for the first time, I did not answer. Unfortunately I can do nothing to hold the *Duce* back. He has decided to act, and act he will. He believes in German success and in the rapidity of this success.

From the *Diary of Count Ciano*, Italian Foreign Minister, 13 May 1940

(a) Study Source A.

From this source and from your own knowledge, explain the reference to 'the Austrian problem'.

[20 marks]

(b) Study Sources C and D.

To what extent do these sources indicate that Mussolini's foreign policy underwent a fundamental change in the years 1939 and 1940? [40 marks]

(c) Study all of the sources.

From these sources, and from your own knowledge, how far would you agree with the claim that 'Mussolini's foreign policy in the 1930s had no consistent principles or aims'? [60 marks]

Source-based questions: The style and substance of Italian Fascism

Study sources 1–5 below and then answer questions (a) and (b) which follow.

SOURCE 1

(From Nicholas Doumanis, *Italy: Inventing the Nation*, published in 2001)

It was the war experience itself, and especially the crisis precipitated by the debacle at Caporetto, that converted many Italians into fully-fledged nationalists. Especially important in galvanising mass support for right-wing nationalism were the 'unpatriotic', disruptive activities of the Left and the Liberal regime's failure to keep the home front in order. Much of bourgeois Italy was therefore attracted to the nationalist rhetoric of the Fascist movement, which outwardly sought to distinguish itself from the Liberal order by conducting a decisive and violent campaign against the Left.

Fascism was principally committed to creating a great nation out of a feeble one, and nationalism was the fundamental basis of its beliefs. The Fascists did not offer a clear political programme, for among their ranks one could find monarchists and republicans, as well as revolutionaries and conservatives, but if anything can be salvaged from their obtuse rhetoric and muddled theories, it was the absolute moral primacy of the nation. It was nationalism that bound this motley cohort together. For the Fascists 'Italia' demanded precedence over class and religion, even family and monarchy. Their challenge was to transmit that passionate fervour for 'Italia' to every Italian regardless of class or gender. As Roberto Farinacci, one of the more radical leaders of the early period once asserted, 'In Italy no one can be an anti-Fascist because an anti-Fascist cannot be an Italian.' The Fascists hoped that they would establish their political legitimacy with a simple rendition of national culture and identity.

SOURCE 2

(From Denis Mack Smith, *Mussolini*, published in 1981)

Mussolini was anxious for the public to think of him as an immensely hard worker, whose working day might last 18 or 19 hours. It was he who suggested to journalists that they might like to spread stories of his industriousness. This legend, like so many others, was false. His staff sometimes had orders to leave a light in his office at night to give the impression that he was working late. He was, in fact, a heavy sleeper who liked going to bed early and staying there for nine hours, not being disturbed even in emergencies. Mussolini was no idler, but the stories of his extraordinary industry and efficiency were exaggerated. He tried to persuade people that he kept up an average of 25 meetings a day throughout the year and that in seven years he had transacted 1,887,112 items of business. This last figure invites suspicion by its characteristic precision and works out at nearly 100 items each hour over a sixty-hour week. Moreover he said that he found time each day for some sporting activity and, each evening, for playing his precious collection of violins. The dramatist Pirandello interpreted Mussolini as being essentially an actor pretending to be the person Italians wanted him to be.

SOURCE 3

(From Martin Clark, *Modern Italy 1871–1982*, published in 1984)

Yet the new political system was not simply the old regime in more authoritarian form. The loss of certain traditional liberties – a free press, free speech, free association – was not trivial, and certainly hurt many members of Italy's former élite: the respectable Liberal anti-Fascists and the Freemasons were the great losers of 1925–26. The price may have been worth paying if it secured law and order, political stability and the maintenance of privilege, but it was still a high price. Moreover, Mussolini was always setting up new institutions and adopting new policies – the battles for wheat and for births, the corporations and the labour tribunals, the youth movements and the Dopolavoro. Many existing state institutions were left largely unchanged, but that is not necessarily proof of continuity of policy. The Fascist government was always innovating, always invading new areas of society and indeed new areas of the world.

Source-based questions: The style and substance of Italian Fascism

SOURCE 4

(From Mussolini's first speech as Prime Minister to the Italian Parliament, November 1922)

Before attaining this position I was asked on all sides for a programme. Alas! It is not programmes that are lacking in Italy; it is the men and the willingness to apply the programmes. All the problems of Italian life, all of them I say, have been solved on paper. What is lacking is the will to translate them into fact. Today the Government represents this firm and decisive will.

SOURCE 5

(From a tract on Fascist beliefs, written by Mussolini in 1934)

The Fascist State is not indifferent to religious phenomena in general, nor does it maintain an attitude of indifference to Roman Catholicism, the special positive religion of the Italians. The Fascist State sees in religion one of the deepest of spiritual manifestations, and for this reason it not only respects religion, but defends and protects it. The Fascist State does not seek, as did Bolshevism, to erase God from the soul of man. Fascism respects the God of monks, saints and heroes, and it also respects God as conceived by the innocent and primitive heart of the people.

Answer both questions (a) and (b).

(a) Using your own knowledge, and the evidence of Sources 1, 2 and 5, what do you consider to have been the main appeal of Fascism to Italians in the 1920s?
[10 marks]

(b) 'For all its claims to be a radical movement, Italian Fascism was mainly a change in political style, and created few significant changes in the social and economic life of Italians.' Using your own knowledge, and the evidence of all five sources, explain how far you agree with this interpretation.
[20 marks]

Further Reading

Texts designed for AS and A2 Level students

Italy: Liberalism and Fascism by Mark Robson (Hodder & Stoughton, Access to History series, 2000)

Mussolini and Fascist Italy by Martin Blinkhorn (Routledge, Lancaster Pamphlets, 1984)

Fascist Italy by John Hite and Chris Hinton (John Murray, Schools History Project, 1998)

More advanced reading

Mussolini by Denis Mack Smith (Weidenfeld & Nicolson, 1981)

Mussolini's Roman Empire by Denis Mack Smith (Penguin, 1977)

Modern Italy 1871–1982 by Martin Clark (Longman, History of Italy series, 1984)

Italian Foreign Policy 1870–1940 by C.J. Lowe and F. Marzari (Routledge & Kegan Paul, 1975)

Fascism in Italy: Society and Culture, 1922–1945 by E.R. Tannenbaum (Allen Lane, 1973)

Fascism in Italy: Its Development and Influence by Elizabeth Wiskemann (Macmillan, 1969)

Index